THE BEST OF
LOIS HOLE

advice & inspiration
FOR GARDENERS

HOLE'S

PUBLISHED BY HOLE'S
  101 Bellerose Drive
  St. Albert, Alberta Canada
  T8N 8N8

Printed in Canada   5   4   3   2   1

Canadian Cataloguing in Publication Data

Hole, Lois, 1933-
  The best of Lois Hole

  ISBN 0-9682791-4-7

  1. Gardening. 2. Gardening—Canada. I. Title.
SB453.3.C2H64 2000   635'.0971   C00-910512-3

Film & Stripping ✻ Elite Lithographers, Edmonton, Alberta, Canada
Printing ✻ Quality Colour Press, Edmonton, Alberta, Canada

Contents

INTRODUCTION ✻ 5

GROW IT FROM SEED! ✻ 8
*Don't be afraid to try starting
your plants from seed indoors.*

TULIP TIME ✻ 11
*Learn a little about the origin of
tulips and how to grow them right.*

PLANTING DATES ✻ 14
*Plant early! Find out why Lois thinks
that you should plant most of your garden
before the "traditional" starting point,
the May long weekend.*

HARDENING OFF ✻ 17
*Lois shows you how to prepare your
plants for the transition from the cozy
indoors to the rough and tumble world
of the outdoor garden.*

BEST OF THE BULBS ✻ 20
*Lois talks about some of her favourite
flowering bulbs, including glads, dinner
plate dahlias, and dahliettas.*

CONTAINER GARDENING
WITH VEGETABLES ✻ 23
*Carrots growing in an old washing
machine? Anything is possible
in the wonderful world of container
vegetable gardening.*

TREE CARE ✻ 26
*Take care of your trees by learning
how to prune and when to consult
a Certified Arborist.*

HANG IN THERE ✻ 29
*Creating a hanging basket that's
overflowing with lush growth is easy.*

GARDENING ON THE FRINGE ✻ 33
*From the unusual but practical to the just
plain bizarre, Lois relates some of her
favourite stories of gardening on the fringe.*

PAVEMENT ROSES ARE
TOUGH AND BEAUTIFUL ✻ 36
*They may look delicate, but pavement
roses are sturdy additions to the garden.*

TWO PATHS ✻ 38
*There's more than one way to deal
with the vagaries of Canada's climate.
Lois describes two different approaches
to handling the weather.*

HUGE TOMATOES ✻ 41
*So, you want to grow the biggest
tomatoes on the block. Lois gives you
the competitive edge you need to get
into the big tomato game.*

SEASONS IN THE SUN ✻ 44
*Lois talks about the effects of sunlight
on plants, from the dangers of
sunscald to how day length influences
blooming times and fruit flavour.*

PESTICIDES ✻ 47
*Lois outlines her philosophy on
pesticide use and describes a number
of bug-control methods.*

A NEW WAY TO IRRIGATE ✻ 51
*Watering is the most important job in the
garden-and there's more than one way to
do it. Lois explains how drip
irrigation saves significant amounts
of our most precious resource.*

GARDEN HARVESTING ✻ 54
*Lois shows you how to harvest vegetables
and berries for the best flavour and
freshness.*

THE COLONELS OF CORN ✻ 57
*What's the difference between normal,
sugar-enhanced, and supersweet corn?
Lois shows you and describes some
of her favourite corn varieties.*

HOT PEPPERS ✻ 60
*Lois' husband Ted discovers that
some peppers are too hot to handle.*

VEGETABLE STORAGE ✻ 63
*Lois' handy storage tips help you
keep your vegetables tasting fresh
for as long as possible.*

THE LIGHT FANTASTIC ✻ 66
*Lois discusses the fascinating effect
of photoperiodism on plants.*

POTTING SOIL POWER ✻ 69
Lois encourages gardeners to give potting soil the respect it deserves. She shows you what to look for in a potting soil, and how important it is to choose the right foundation for proper growth.

SEED TECHNOLOGY ✻ 72
Lois explains how seed companies determine which seed varieties are winners and which don't make the grade.

THINKING SMALL ✻ 75
Check out these cool dwarf varieties of some of your favourite plants. Lois discusses bonsai, dwarf apple trees, and dwarf sunflowers.

ZONAL GERANIUMS
ALL YEAR ROUND ✻ 78
You can keep your geraniums all year long by moving them indoors for the winter. Here's how.

NEW VARIETIES DON'T
GROW ON TREES ✻ 81
Lois tells the story of the New Guinea Impatiens, from its discovery to modern breeding techniques.

A CAUTIONARY TALE
OF HERBAL MEDICINES ✻ 84
Echinacea has become a popular cure-all. But does the bottle you buy on the shelf contain the genuine article?

FALLING OUT OF FAVOR ✻ 87
The Favor carrot was one of Lois' favourites, but now it's gone. Lois explains why the best varieties sometimes fade away despite their outstanding quality.

HYBRID SEEDS ✻ 90
Lois discusses the origins and advantages of hybrid seed.

HIGH-TECH GARDENING ✻ 93
Lois discusses some of the latest gardening gizmos, including a point and shoot thermometer and the amazing plant stress detection glasses.

LET THERE BE LIGHTS ✻ 96
Supplemental lighting can help your plants thrive when daylight grows scarce. Find out which grow lights do the job best.

THE SECRET LIVES
OF GERANIUMS ✻ 99
Lois explains the difference between seed and cloned geraniums and tells the fascinating story of their propagation.

YOU SAY TOMATO…
BUT IS IT? ✻ 102
Lois reveals the secret of the "tomato tree" and shows how knowing a little Latin and having an adventurous spirit can enhance your enjoyment of gardening.

THE $10,000 HOSTA ✻ 105
Lois discusses the amazing lengths people will go to to collect rare plants. But would anyone really pay $10,000 for a hosta?

A PEAR OF GREAT PRICE ✻ 108
Heirloom varieties are treasures, full of priceless genetic information that must be preserved for future generations. Lois tells the story of the rescue of a rare pear variety.

CAUTIOUS CANADIANS ✻ 111
What caused a farmer's pants to catch on fire? Find out, and learn about the process of registering chemicals for garden use in Canada.

THE GARDENERS OF
THE GOLDEN AGE ✻ 114
Discover how legendary plant breeder Robert Simonet unlocked the secret of growing double-flowering petunias from seed, and learn about how plant breeders patent new varieties.

BOULEVARD OF DREAMS ✻ 118
Boulevard trees are a precious community resource…here's how to care for them.

ANOTHER APPROACH ✻ 121
Lois tells the story of her May 1999 trip to Tokyo, and shows how Canadian and Japanese gardeners have influenced each other.

A FEAST FOR THE SENSES ✻ 124
Gardens appeal not just to sight and smell…there's something for all the senses.

ABOUT THE AUTHOR ✻ 128

Introduction

Between February 1997 and September 1999, I wrote gardening columns for the *Globe & Mail*. Every three weeks, one of my short commentaries appeared in the *Globe's* weekend Focus section. The chance to share some advice and inspiration with a diverse audience was invigorating, and it gave me the opportunity to explore the evolution of horticultural trends. That exploration turned out to be even more educational than I expected, giving me new insights into many aspects of gardening.

The people who asked me about gardening used to fit the stereotype: older, affluent folks. But now gardeners are from all kinds of economic and ethnic backgrounds, and there are many more young people discovering the pursuit. I welcome this diversity and expect the trend to continue—indeed, I think it's the cornerstone of the blossoming popularity of gardening.

Perhaps not surprisingly, this explosion of interest comes as life's complexity increases. I found that as free time grows scarce and life becomes more hectic, instant gratification is becoming more attractive than ever. Gardening, a once-stately, laid-back hobby, is not immune to the need for speed. More gardeners than ever are buying large plants with full blooms from greenhouses so that they can enjoy an "instant garden." (That's not so new. I remember a fellow who bought the biggest fully grown tomato plant in the greenhouse every year. He then planted it and told his neighbours he'd raised it from seed.)

But speed isn't paramount for all gardeners; some cherish uniqueness. Collecting has enjoyed a surge in popularity, whether it be bottlecaps, baseball cards, or unique alpine perennials. There are plenty of rare, expensive plants to whet the collector's appetite—trees, roses, peonies, even a one-of-a-kind Japanese hosta appraised at an amazing $10,000. But you don't have to be rich to showcase one or two unique varieties in your yard: there are some for every price bracket.

On a related note, I've been peppered with requests for information about strange, exotic plants like the "tomato tree" and the "indoor banana tree." The ads promise basketfuls of fruit, but could any plant live up to such hype? Does it need to? I've found that sometimes the rewards of growing unusual plants are not those that are advertised, but that's not necessarily bad. Looking beyond the hype to find the truth is as important in today's gardening as it is in today's media.

New hybrid varieties, on the other hand, are generally performing up to expectations. Hybrids are getting a lot of attention, and rightly so: their characteristics are generally superior to the old heirloom varieties. But heirloom plants still have an indispensable place in gardening, and we should take care to preserve the best of the older varieties.

In embracing the old, though, we shouldn't shun the new. While I'm not very adept at handling electronics, I do recognize that the role of technology is expanding in gardening. I expect more and more gardens to feature at least one or two high-tech tools—

perhaps a pair of plant stress-detection glasses or, in the future, a "garden health monitor" that will let you know when your dahlias need watering.

Advances in technology in fields beyond horticulture still affect gardening trends. Thanks to the influence of immigration, television, the Internet, and books, traditional medicinal plants are enjoying a surge in popularity. While we've enjoyed old standards like garlic and mint for ages, Canadian gardens are slowly being infiltrated with exotic herbs like shiso, epazote, red orach, and many others. The medicinal uses of these plants and many others are in vogue right now—although their benefits may vary widely, as does their acceptance by the public and professional horticulturists.

Several months have passed since the last article I wrote for the *Globe*, "Boulevard of Dreams," was published. It's been an incredible learning experience. The stories, when taken together, chronicle my thoughts on the changes in gardening in the closing years of the Twentieth century. I certainly didn't have such an agenda in mind when I started submitting articles to the *Globe*, but the result is a pleasant, if unexpected, outcome. It's become obvious to me that a global gardening culture is developing, one that employs the best elements from each national tradition.

It's been a privilege to participate in the evolution of Canadian gardening. I can't wait to see what the future brings.

Lois E. Hole
June, 2000

━━━ BEST ADVICE ━━━
for starting seed indoors...
Professional seedling mix • Bottom heat • A sunny window

DURING THE DARK DAYS OF WINTER, ONE OF MY FAVOURITE PASTIMES
IS TO FLIP THROUGH THE PAGES OF THE SEED CATALOGUES. I REALLY
FIND IT EXCITING–THE ANTICIPATION, THE CURIOSITY. WILL THAT
PEA OR TOMATO REALLY TURN OUT TO BE AS DELICIOUS AS IT LOOKS
IN THE PICTURE? THANK GOODNESS WE CAN START SEED INDOORS
AND GET A BIT OF A JUMP ON THE GARDENING SEASON.
OTHERWISE, I'D GO CRAZY WAITING FOR SPRING TO ARRIVE.

Grow It from Seed!

⚜ ORIGINALLY PUBLISHED FEBRUARY 1, 1997 ⚜

Quick, which would you rather have: an ounce of gold or an
ounce of begonia seed? Gold at its current market price of
around $300 an ounce is mere pocket change compared to a series
of tuberous begonia seed called 'Charisma' that rings in at an
astounding $200,000 an ounce.

Mind you, an ounce of begonia seed does contain anywhere
from 1.5 to 2 million seeds and, in all fairness, only the world's
largest plant propagators would ever buy an ounce.

Thankfully for home gardeners, growing your own plants from
seed is substantially less expensive. It can also be an incredibly
rewarding experience, but at other times it can be just downright
frustrating.

I remember when my husband Ted and I first got started in market gardening back in the early 1960s. We needed a large number of tomato transplants and obviously that required a greenhouse, so we built one—a small, plastic-covered, wood-framed structure.

Having very little seed experience, I rationalized that if I sowed double the recommended number of tomato seeds I should, at the very least, get half to grow and therefore be pretty darn close to my target.

After about a month, not one seedling had emerged. Of course, I blamed everything and everyone, including my husband, for this abysmal failure, but it wasn't until Ted decided to check the soil temperature that he was finally exonerated. The soil temperature was a rather frigid 50°F (that was in the pre-metric days) and tomatoes, being warm season plants, prefer a nice warm 70°F, or 21°C to germinate properly. Installation of some heating cable solved that problem for us, but for many gardeners, poor control of soil temperature is still the primary reason for poor results.

Each year more and more gardeners are starting their own seeds, which I'm sure has been fuelled in part by the tremendous satisfaction derived from successfully nurturing a plant from seed to maturity.

Undoubtedly, the adventure of trying the new, the improved, and the unusual is a strong motivator as well, and never before has there been such an extensive selection of seeds.

Yet for many gardeners, there still exists an unwarranted fear of growing seedlings. So to minimize the trauma of starting seed, here is the seed starter's primer in one highly condensed, non-technical paragraph.

The first thing to do is purchase only high-quality seed (which is typically a little more expensive). Place the seed in a tray on top of pre-moistened soilless seedling mixture. Cover the seed lightly with horticultural grade vermiculite (that's the small stuff). Mist the seed tray several times with a pump bottle. Cover the tray with a clear or opaque plastic cover and place the whole apparatus on a heat register or heating cables as close as possible to a south-facing window. Inspect the seed daily and mist as required.

That's all there is to it. Most seed fits rather neatly within these parameters, although, of course, there are those seeds that deviate somewhat. Some like the soil a little warmer or a little cooler, some like a little more or a little less moisture, but the same basic principles still apply.

Still, there are some plant species, particularly a few perennials, that can be rather obstinate. Some perennial seeds require a treatment called stratification—a 1 to 4-month cold treatment in moist soil to break the seeds' self-imposed dormancy. Other perennial seeds must be scarified, which is essentially a delicate cutting or etching of the seed coat to allow germination, allowing water to be drawn in.

I remember a few particularly stubborn perennial seeds that I've tried to germinate in the greenhouse. One in particular was the Himalayan Blue poppy.

After my disappointing experience with tomato seed, I must admit that I leaned on the warm side for starting all other seedlings, including poppies. After about six weeks of tender care, the poppies, like the tomatoes, had failed to emerge, so in frustration I just pulled the trays off the heating cables, left them on the cold floor, and forgot about them. Inadvertently, I had provided exactly what the poppies wanted—a nice, cool spot—and within days the tiny seedlings were popping up.

If you have seed left over when all of the spring seeding is said and done and you're wondering just what is the best way to store it, just remember the rule of 100. Any combination of relative humidity percentage and air temperature that exceeds 100 will reduce seed storage life. For example, if the air temperature is 60°F (sorry, this rule only works with Fahrenheit, not Celsius) and the relative humidity is 40%, you're in the correct range. However, if the relative humidity climbs to 60%, then the air temperature shouldn't exceed 40°F to maintain the 100 rule. The lower the number drops below 100, the better.

If you have a bright window, some heat, and a little patience, give starting your own seed a try. Remember, all that glistens is not gold.

Best Advice
for growing tulips...
Plant early • Purchase big bulbs • Plant in cluster of at least 5

AS I WRITE THIS INTRODUCTION IN EARLY MAY 2000, MANY OF THE TULIPS
WE PLANTED IN OUR GARDEN ARE ALREADY UP AND FLOWERING, AND
I CAN'T WAIT FOR THE OTHERS TO CATCH UP. I WAS INSPIRED TO WRITE
THIS ARTICLE BECAUSE OUR FRIEND HANS FROM PARIDON HORTICULTURAL
HAD JUST SENT US A PICTURE OF AN AMAZING NEW 3-TONED TULIP
CALLED CELEBRATION. THOUGH AVAILABILITY WAS LIMITED AT THE TIME,
I COULDN'T WAIT TO WRITE ABOUT CELEBRATION, AND THAT GAVE ME
THE CHANCE TO PASS ALONG A LITTLE INFORMATION ABOUT THE HISTORY
AND CULTIVATION OF TULIPS. OH YES, I SHOULD MENTION THAT
CELEBRATION IS NOW MUCH EASIER TO OBTAIN. PLANT A FEW THIS FALL!

Tulip Time

✤ORIGINALLY PUBLISHED SEPTEMBER 27 , 1997 ✤

I can see why, for the past 400 or so years, the Dutch have been
so enamoured with the tulip. Few other plants can match the tulip's
flawless, smooth foliage and clean, bright flowers.

Tulips, however, are indigenous not to Holland but rather to the
steppe regions of western and central Asia. The Turks introduced the
tulip to the Dutch, who adopted it as their own. Still, the Dutch
can take a tremendous amount of credit for breeding the tulip and
creating many of the varieties that are grown today.

With the first crisp, cool days of autumn, gardeners are irrepressibly drawn to the tulip bulb displays, just to see what new varieties are available. Although the time to plant them is now, the window for planting tulips in the fall is rather wide. On the prairies, any time from September until mid October is just fine, while in regions with milder late-fall weather, planting can extend well into November.

Once the tulips have been planted, they require very little additional care. They are prone to very few insect pests or diseases, require little water, and are really only bothered by the odd thieving squirrel or occasional deer. However, what is essential for bulb growth is proper temperature. Once the bulbs are planted in the fall into cool, moist soil, they immediately begin producing new roots and initiating some growth of the tiny leaves and the flower bud that formed prior to the bulbs being harvested.

At this point, the bulb enters a state of suspended animation that can only be broken by a prolonged chilling period. Fortunately, in Canada, this chilling period never fails to arrive: it's called winter, and it's more than enough chilling to break the tulips out of dormancy and cause growth to resume in the spring.

After about 15 or so weeks of chilling, the tulips will begin growing immediately if the weather warms to at least 10°C. That's why on the west coast tulips may begin sprouting in late January, while in the chinook belt of Alberta, tulips will begin popping up in February after a prolonged spell of warm chinook weather.

Although chilling of tulips is never a problem here in Canada, choosing which varieties to plant can be a formidable question because the selection is really quite astounding. There are somewhere around 14 divisions of tulips, with each division containing numerous varieties.

Those in division 1 are what many people would describe as the quintessential tulips: classically cup-shaped, single-flowered and emerging from pointed buds. For gardeners who find division 1 tulips far too mundane, division 7, or 'Parrot', tulips may just be the answer. With their fringed, ruffled, flaming flowers, these tulips are truly a novelty. They also make wonderful cut-flowers.

Unquestionably the most striking tulip to come along in years is called 'Celebration'. It's from the 'Triumph' group (division 3) and was recently introduced to the marketplace with considerable pomp and ceremony—and for good reason. When Celebration first sprouted from the soil in the Netherlands, it did so inconspicuously: just standard tulip foliage and red petals. However, once the petals unfolded, the plant breeders were stunned to see that the flower had an incredibly beautiful blue iridescent centre ringed with a delicate bright-white line. The availability of Celebration this fall is somewhat limited, but well worth the search.

If you're planting a few tulips this fall, remember one important rule: buy only the biggest bulbs. Bargain-priced bulbs are often undersized and will either produce inferior quality flowers next spring or not flower at all. Big bulbs quite simply produce bigger, better flowers. The highest-quality bulbs are labelled as 12+, meaning that all of the bulbs in that particular package are a minimum of 12 cm in circumference, while bargain bulbs often have a circumference of only 9 to 11 cm.

If you've never tried growing tulips in pots, give it a shot this fall. Use light, clean potting soil to ensure good bulb growth and to allow for easy transport of the pots. In mild winter regions, the pots can simply be left on the patio, exposed to winter weather; but in cold winter regions, the pots must be protected and light enough to be easily moved to a sheltered area. On the prairies, pots must be thoroughly covered with a mulching material like peat moss to insulate against the cold.

In early April, the pots should be placed in a warm, sunny spot on the patio to encourage rapid growth. And don't be concerned if the temperature suddenly drops in April. I've seen fully emerged tulips withstand temperatures of -16°C and continue to grow and bloom completely unscathed. I can't believe any plant this tough doesn't have at least a little bit of Canadian blood!

BEST ADVICE
on choosing planting dates...
Plant early • Plant late • Plant often

WHILE WE WERE PREPARING THIS BOOK, THE TEMPERATURE PLUMMETED TO -12 DEGREES CELSIUS-AND WE'D ALREADY PLANTED MANY OF OUR VEGETABLES AND FLOWERS. BUT WAS I WORRIED? NOT ON YOUR LIFE! IF WE'D LIVED BY THAT OLD "WAIT UNTIL AFTER MAY 24TH TO PLANT" RULE, THE GREENHOUSE WOULD HAVE GONE OUT OF BUSINESS LONG, LONG AGO. THE TRUTH IS, THERE ARE MANY PLANTS YOU CAN GET INTO THE GROUND EVEN BEFORE THE LAST PILES OF SNOW HAVE COMPLETELY MELTED AWAY.

Planting Dates

ↂ ORIGINALLY PUBLISHED APRIL 12, 1997 ↂ

I grimace a little each time I hear someone say, "I never plant my vegetable garden until after the May long weekend." Could it be that malevolent Mother Nature has a vendetta against gardeners that miraculously expires sometime shortly after Queen Victoria's birthday?

I'm sure that for the many gardeners who have endured late April or early May snowfalls, the answer would be a resounding yes. But once you've accepted the capricious nature of early spring weather in Canada, particularly on the prairies, and you've tried planting early, then the fear of planting in April tends to diminish somewhat. And besides, only early planting will satisfy the main objective of all vegetable gardeners: to enjoy the incomparable taste and texture of fresh vegetables for as long as is humanly possible.

Fortunately, most vegetables are remarkably well adapted to fluctuating temperatures. Broccoli, peas, onions, lettuce, and spinach in particular are extremely frost tolerant. I've often sown these vegetables during gloriously warm, early April days and watched the seedlings poke through the rich black soil a few days later only to have a late blast of cold arctic air plunge temperatures far below freezing. Yet these resilient vegetables remain unscathed by the cold and shrug off temperatures approaching a chilly -8°C. Vegetables like beets, carrots, and cauliflower, although not quite as frost hardy, are still quite capable of enduring several degrees of frost.

But what about vegetables that are sensitive to frost? Are they worth planting early?

Two frost-sensitive vegetables in particular—corn and potatoes—help to answer this question. In the event of even a light frost, the above-ground growth is rapidly flattened. But since corn has a growing point that remains below ground until its foliage is at least 10 cm tall, even if a frost injures the top growth, new shoots rapidly emerge within days. Potatoes will produce a multitude of new shoots very rapidly after a hard frost has blackened exposed foliage. For both corn and potatoes, these subterranean shoots are probably adaptations to foraging animals and hungry insects, and fortunately for gardeners, this adaptation has inadvertently provided a certain degree of protection against frost.

Now, if we continue to move down the list, starting with vegetables that are "frost hardy," it's inevitable that we are going to run smack into those vegetables that will perish with even the slightest touch of frost. Standing front and centre are members of the cucurbit family: cucumbers, squash, and melons. Tomatoes aren't far behind. Should they be planted early?

Well, undeniably, these very frost-sensitive vegetables haven't a hope if they are exposed for any length of time to temperatures even slightly below 0°C, but this is where the early-planting issue changes course somewhat.

Let's forget the frost sensitivity of these plants for a moment but keep in mind that the main objective of growing vegetables is to enjoy them for as long as possible.

Say, for example, that you plant four dollars' worth of cucumber seeds and four dollars' worth of tomato transplants sometime in late April. If the temperatures fall faster than Bre-X stock, than you're still out only about eight dollars' worth of seed and plants (plus, of course, your time spent planting). There is still plenty of time for re-planting, and as long as your enthusiasm is still intact, you should be right back on track. If, on the other hand, the weather remains nice and warm, the plants will enjoy a much longer growing season and respond with substantially higher yields. That risky eight-dollar investment begins to pay substantial dividends.

However, if you find that reducing vegetable gardening down to nothing more than a cost/benefit analysis borders on the sacrilegious—after all, we are talking about living things—then you might want to try a gardening technique that is absolutely guaranteed to protect even the most tender vegetables from any degree of cold. Each April, a close friend of mine carefully plants his cucumbers and tomatoes in old 22-litre buckets. The buckets are placed on a special 4-wheeled cart that he pushes onto his deck during the day, weather permitting. At night, if there is an impending frost, he simply wheels the cart into his garage. No waking up in the middle of the night to check the temperature, no blankets draped over the tomatoes, just a good night's sleep.

Canada is blessed with many wonderful attributes, but for most of its regions, an extremely long growing season isn't one of them. This April, throw caution to the wind. Walk out to the garden, rope off a portion of the plot, and try planting some of your vegetables early—live dangerously!

——— BEST ADVICE ———
when hardening off plants...
Keep it cool • Don't overwater • Keep it sunny

I WROTE THIS COLUMN BECAUSE "HARDENING OFF" IS A TERM USED BY MANY PROFESSIONAL HORTICULTURISTS BUT OFTEN CONFUSED WITH "HARDINESS" BY LESS-EXPERIENCED GARDENERS. SINCE HARDENING OFF IS SO CRUCIAL TO THE HEALTH OF MANY STORE-BOUGHT YOUNG PLANTS, I WANTED MY READERS TO KNOW THAT THEY SHOULD ALWAYS SEEK OUT HARDENED-OFF PLANTS.

Hardening Off

ORIGINALLY PUBLISHED MAY 2, 1998

Not too long ago, my husband Ted and I were asked to attend a gardening seminar in New Orleans. This was towards the end of January, and at home the weather was frigid; not only could you see your breath, it practically turned to ice and fell at your feet. Well, when we landed in New Orleans, I just about died: the heat hit in suffocating waves, making me very uncomfortable. It probably wasn't really that hot, but going through such a difference in temperatures without adequate preparation made it tough for my body to adjust. Everyone has had experiences like this; even stepping out of a hot tub into a relatively cool room can produce this uncomfortable shock. It's much nicer when we have a chance to gradually adjust to different temperatures.

Plants are subject to this phenomenon too, but to a greater extent. While humans might be made uncomfortable by rapid changes in temperature, plants can die from it. They can, however, be protected from damage by being acclimatized to a cooler environment. This process of acclimatization is called hardening off.

In the early spring, when plants are transplanted from your home into the garden, they are moving from an environment with low light and warm temperatures (and often high humidity) to one with lots of light and comparatively cooler temperatures; it may also be drier. If you move a plant from one extreme to the other without preparing it for the change, you risk damaging it. Unconditioned plants have weak, soft stems and leaves; they are very prone to disease, cold, and sunburn.

To avoid this unhappy condition, here at the greenhouse we germinate seeds and root cuttings in soil at 20 to 24°C, then move them to a cooler area where it's around 16 to 18°C, and finally to 12 to 14°C before selling them to the public. We also have fans that keep the air in the greenhouse moving; this simulates the effect of wind on plants, which increases leaf and stem thickness. The result is tougher, more resilient plants that are much more likely to thrive in the garden. The vast majority of garden plants benefit from cool conditioning; pansies, violas, snapdragons, and petunias respond especially well to this treatment. However, even heat-loving plants like tomatoes can benefit from cool air. A week or two of temperatures in the low teens causes the early onset of flowering, leading to earlier fruitset and a greater yield overall. Note, however, that warm-season vegetable crops like cucumbers, melons, and squash benefit more from air movement than cooling; they can suffer chilling injury if they are kept at temperatures in the 8°C range for a prolonged period of time.

If you're growing plants from seed inside your home for transplanting, you can harden them off by placing them outside on the deck during the day in a shady, sheltered spot and bringing them indoors at night. After a period of about seven to ten days, you can transplant them into your garden. Putting them immediately into direct sunlight, without this hardening-off period, almost invariably results in sunburn on the leaves. If you're using small containers like sixpacks, make sure that they are thoroughly watered; small containers are prone to drying out.

It's easy to tell the difference between hardened and unhardened plants. Hardened plants are bushy and stocky, with dark-green leaves that don't flop or sag. In sharp contrast, unhardened plants are tall, pale, and floppy.

Be sure to leave sufficient space between the plants during all stages of plant growth. Overcrowding causes stretched, soft plants; this is because of competition for sunlight. Rapid but soft growth results when a plant's leaves are shaded by a neighbouring plant's leaves. In an effort to get more sunlight, the plant shoots upward, attempting to escape the shade. Of course, the first plant responds in the same way; in the end, you will have a bunch of tall, spindly plants that are more likely to die than stockier, more robust plants.

Give your plants a chance to thrive. Let them get used to the conditions of the great outdoors before letting them loose in the wild.

Speaking of the cold, there are some plants that don't need hardening off, like evergreen shrubs. I especially like the new rhododendron varieties from the University of Helsinki in Finland. These amazing plants can survive cold as extreme as -36°C! If you're looking to try out one of these tough and gorgeous shrubs, look for these names: 'Haaga,' 'Heilikki,' 'Mikkeli,' and 'Peter Tigerstedt.' They have absolutely beautiful flowers in a variety of traditional rhododendron colours, and they will add some green to your yard all year long. What could be better?

Alpines are another hardy group of perennials that look great in the garden. Saxifrage makes attractive ground cover, with bright red, pink, and white flowers; it's a good choice for rock gardens or for planting along paths. Gentians form lovely carpets of true blue (not the more common purple) flowers; they're great for borders or edging. Alpine woodruff and lewisia are other good alpine perennials with lovely pink and white flowers, respectively. All of these varieties have been thoroughly tested for hardiness; they are very well adapted to fluctuating temperatures.

Unpredictable weather doesn't have to interfere with the enjoyment of your garden. A little preparation and knowledge of your plants goes a long way towards success.

——— BEST ADVICE———
for planting bulbs...
Start with rich soil • Provide good drainage • Plant top-quality bulbs

THE DEMAND FOR BULB INFORMATION HAS BEEN GROWING AT SUCH A
RATE THAT I'VE FINALLY DECIDED TO START WORK ON A BOOK ABOUT
BULBS.LOOK FOR IT IN 2001. UNTIL THEN, HERE'S A BRIEF LOOK AT SOME
OF THE BEST BULBS AROUND-THERE'S ONE FOR EVERY TASTE AND BUDGET.

Best of the Bulbs

✿ ORIGINALLY PUBLISHED MARCH 21, 1998 ✿

Is it a bulb, a tuber, or a corm? Most of us probably apply these
terms correctly to the corresponding plants, but few of us get it
right all of the time.

The catch-all term for plants that utilize some sort of under-
ground storage organ is *geophyte.* But since geophyte is a rather pon-
derous term, and likely to draw a blank from nursery staff should
you ask for the "geophyte section," feel free, if you like, to yield to
the masses and just call them all bulbs.

In most regions of Canada, excluding the west coast, which is
already miles ahead of the rest of us in terms of sprouting plants,
fall-planted bulbs like tulips are just beginning to pop out of the
soil. And since their fate is by and large determined by the quality
of bulbs that were planted last fall, it's just a matter of sitting back
and enjoying their glorious blooms in the weeks to come.

The emergence of the fall-planted bulbs coincides nicely with the arrival of the tender bulbs in the nurseries. And although there seems to be ample time, since it is only late March, the selection dwindles fairly rapidly as the bulb aficionados scoop up the hot new varieties.

One of the most popular spring-planted bulbs (corms, actually) is gladiolus with its spires of radiant flowers. There are essentially four categories of gladiolus: standards, dwarfs, landscape, and American hybrids. The American hybrids are perhaps the most spectacular, just because of their size. The spikes will often reach nearly five and a half feet, and most of the flowers open simultaneously, which is a wonderful trait for spectacular bouquets. I've found that the biggest-flowered, tallest-spiked glads invariably grow in the richest, deepest soils and areas that receive direct sunlight from dawn to dusk. A little shade shouldn't preclude you from growing American hybrids, but just be aware that they won't be quite as majestic as their full-sun kin.

The standards are not quite as tall as the American hybrid, but I think they are equal in beauty. Standard glads are usually about six or so inches shorter than the American hybrids, but nonetheless, varieties in this category like 'Peach Parfait' and 'Blooming Orange' have flowers that are just as spectacular.

Landscape glads appeal to those of us who are truly enamoured with the gladiolus but hate the idea of having to stake the darn things. They are quite a bit smaller than either the standards or the Americans, attaining a height of about three and a half feet, but they have the strength to stand up without any support other than their own sturdy stems. I love the variety 'Florida' because of its sunny yellow petals blotched with red in the centre.

Dwarf gladioli are the smallest of all the categories and wonderfully suited to those gardeners with limited space. They seldom grow taller than one foot, but their flowers are certainly equal in beauty to any other gladioli. There is one series of dwarfs that is a rather distinct departure from all of the others, called orchid gladioli. The orchid name is derived from the orchid-like flowers on the gladiolus spikes. 'Prins Claus' is unquestionably my favourite variety because its flowers have the most striking similarity to those of true orchids. Each flower typically has four small petals splashed with red, offset by two large, pure-white petals on the opposite side—truly a remarkable flower.

Few other plants have such a wide variety of colours, flower forms, and height as the dahlia. And indeed, few others are as versatile. Tall dahlias are excellent for specimen plantings, while the shorter varieties are terrific as bedding plants or compact growers for containers. Dahlias continue to bloom over the entire summer and are also great as cut-flowers.

This year, save at least one spot in your garden for dinnerplate dahlias. The flower heads are absolutely massive! I have yet to grow one with flowers the same diameter as a dinner plate, but I've grown many that are at least eight inches across. The key to growing these plants successfully is to give them a pinch of 20-20-20 fertilizer at each watering and, like the glads, lots of sunlight. The plants grow about three feet tall, so plenty of space is a prerequisite.

Two dinnerplates that I really enjoy growing are 'Angel Face' and 'Yvonne'. Angel Face has flowers with bright-red centres frosted with white-tipped petals, while Yvonne is rose highlighted with peach.

I'm really eager to try a new series called the 'Super' dinnerplate dahlias. The plants grow to the same height as regular dinnerplate dahlias, but the flowers are purported to be about two inches wider.

Moving down the scale in size are the standard dahlias. Standards contain a number of subcategories or series with a remarkable range of forms and colours. For example, a series called waterlily dahlias do indeed resemble the flowers of pond waterlilies and range in colour from white to pale lavender.

If dinnerplates and standard dahlias are too big for your yard, consider dahliettas. These little dahlias seldom grow taller than a foot yet are exceptionally floriferous and compact. They are vegetatively propagated, meaning that they are not produced from seed. Rather, cuttings were taken from a superior mother plant variety and multiplied to produce identical offspring. What this means is that if you buy, say, a 'Royal Beauty' dahlietta tuber in Vancouver, it will be genetically identical to a 'Royal Beauty' tuber in St. John's.

Regardless of the bulbs, tubers, corms, or whatever other geophytes you buy this spring, remember that the size of the storage structure is the greatest predictor of garden performance. Choose only the largest, blemish-free bulbs from within each category. The secret to success is indeed buried beneath your feet.

———— BEST ADVICE ————
for growing vegetables in containers...
Big containers • Regular fertilizer • Lots of water

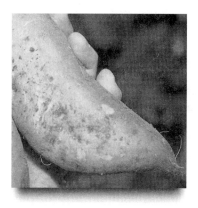

MY FRIENDS THE FARLEYS SOLD THEIR HOUSE AND MOVED INTO AN
APARTMENT WITH A SMALL BALCONY. THEY LOVED THEIR NEW PLACE,
BUT THEY REGRETTED THE LOSS OF THEIR BIG GARDEN. "WE CAN'T
GROW ROOT VEGETABLES ANYMORE, AND I MISS MY BEET TOPS!"
"WELL, SURE YOU CAN GROW ROOT CROPS ON THE BALCONY!"
I SAID, AND AS I EXPLAINED HOW, I REALIZED THAT OTHER
APARTMENT DWELLERS–AND CONVENTIONAL GARDENERS!
MIGHT BE ABLE TO USE THE INFORMATION TOO.

Container Gardening with Vegetables

✢ ORIGINALLY PUBLISHED JUNE 14, 1997 ✢

It's not until you actually see carrots growing in an old, beat-up washing machine that you truly appreciate the determination and ingenuity of gardeners.

This past summer a friend of mine, who has a very tiny garden, filled his 25-year-old washing machine with potting soil and tossed in a package of Nantes 616 carrots. By late July, he had harvested enough beautiful, crisp, clean carrots to fill a large plastic bag.

I must admit that although my taste in pots and planters is much more traditional, I still love to experiment with new and sometimes unusual vegetables in containers.

23

This past summer I received some information on growing sweet potatoes from a producer in New Brunswick. I purchased a few Georgia Jet sweet potato cuttings from him and in March planted them into four-inch pots in our greenhouses. By late May the cuttings were well rooted, and I placed four plants each in three oak half-barrels. Considering that sweet potatoes are more commonly grown in the deep American South, I covered each plant with a clear plastic hot cap to provide a nice, warm environment and encourage vigorous growth.

Surprisingly enough, with the exception of one sweet potato plant that rotted shortly after transplanting, the others grew remarkably well during our abnormally cool and cloudy summer, and by late August each plant developed on average three large, deep-orange-fleshed tubers. In fact, one barrel produced seventeen tubers from only four plants.

If I had to choose one group of plants that I enjoy testing in containers, it has to be the tomato. Tomatoes are exceptionally well suited to container growing. One of my favorites is Tumbler, a variety that is extremely prolific and one that I've had tremendous success with in twelve-inch hanging baskets. No other tomato variety produces such an abundance of fruit from such a small plant.

Jean Irwin, a close friend of mine, grew two tumblers and had enough fruit to supply her family of four all summer long. What's more remarkable is that, with the exception of one, all of the family members are tomato-loving vegetarians.

The Tumbler's mature fruit is typically golf-ball size, as long as the plants are fed heavily once a week with a fertilizer like 20-20-20; otherwise, the subsequent fruit is no bigger than a grape.

I still enjoy iceberg or romaine lettuce salads, but the trend toward the more exotic blends of plant varieties is one that is particularly well suited to container gardening and is long overdue. Mesclun is a blend of leafy greens that has been very popular in Europe and gaining in popularity in North America. There are in fact many different mesclun blends, and I've tried about six different types in the garden. The one that I've found to be the best for containers includes a combination of mustard spinach, mustard greens, edible chrysanthemum, lamb's quarters, arugula, coriander, lettuce, radish, spinach, and chervil.

Mesclun is best sown in early spring since most of the mesclun species prefer cool, sunny weather. During hot weather, provide some afternoon shade and always harvest in the morning when the air is cool; otherwise the leaves tend to wilt. Mesclun should be harvested en masse by clipping off the tops when the plants are about five to eight centimetres tall.

Over the past couple of years, I've had tremendous success growing strawberries in hanging towers. Strawberry towers are simply green plastic tubes, one foot in diameter, with a saucer on one end and hooks on the other. The tube is filled with soilless mixture and the strawberry plants are pushed into evenly spaced holes in the tube. One strawberry variety that is absolutely wonderful in towers is Tri-Star.

Tri-Star is a day-neutral strawberry that has outstanding flavour and produces very heavy yields. Day neutrals, unlike traditional strawberry varieties, do not require long days for fruit production. I've found that in the Edmonton region, the heaviest fruiting occurs in late July and continues right up until a heavy fall frost. A weekly feeding of soil fertilizer like 15-15-30 is essential considering the large number of plants in a relatively small volume of soil. The ripe fruit is extremely sweet but exceptionally delicate and should be removed from the plant very carefully. Since the fruit is so fragile, it is best eaten fresh. Not surprisingly, few berries ever make it to the kitchen.

If you have very little garden space, consider growing vegetables in containers. All you really need is a little imagination—and perhaps an old washing machine.

——— BEST ADVICE ———
on choosing good pruners...
Strong steel • Replaceable parts • Comfortable grip

DURING THE STORM MENTIONED IN THIS ARTICLE, WE LOST A HUGE
BRANCH FROM THE VENERABLE OLD MAPLE TREE IN FRONT OF OUR HOUSE.
THE LOSS WAS VERY UPSETTING–WE'D HAD THE TREE FOR DECADES, AND
THE LOST BRANCH WAS THE ONE WITH THE TIRE SWING ON IT.
A LOT OF MEMORIES WERE WRAPPED UP IN THAT LOST LIMB, BUT AT LEAST
THE DAMAGE TO OUR TREE GAVE ME THE CHANCE TO PASS ON SOME
IMPORTANT TIPS ABOUT TREE CARE TO MY FELLOW GARDENERS.

Tree Care

⤞ ORIGINALLY PUBLISHED FEBRUARY 7, 1997 ⤝

Early one morning last spring, I awoke to the sound of tree limbs
cracking and crashing to the ground. Tree leaves laden with heavy,
wet snow were far too great a burden for the limbs to bear, and
the streets and backyards were soon strewn with branches and
fallen trees. The Edmonton storm was quite localized and pales
in comparison to the enormous ice storm in the east, but the
clean-up is the same. And once the fallen limbs and debris are
cleared, then what?

Last year when my favourite tree, a large Manitoba maple, lost a
limb during the storm, I sought the advice of Phil Croteau. Phil a

member of our staff, is a certified arborist—one who specializes in the art and science of growing and managing trees.

Phil explained that the emotional attachment we have to our shade trees clouds our objectivity when they are injured. Anyone who has a majestic shade tree will likely be appalled at the notion of sawing its limbs or removing it, even if it is severely damaged. But, as Phil explained, emotions must yield to reason at a certain point, because even the most beloved trees can be hazardous.

The arborist's definition of a hazardous tree is one with a high potential for toppling or losing a limb, coupled with its proximity to objects it could hit, like homes, garages, or playgrounds. Hazardous-tree assessment is rather difficult because the evaluation is somewhat subjective. Even the most skilled arborist cannot predict exactly when a tree limb will crack and fall.

Certified arborists have a standardized tree-hazard evaluation form that comprehensively lists every characteristic of a tree that could cause it to fall. Starting with obvious information like the species name, the form lists everything from trunk taper to cracks, exposed roots, and even whether it has a bird-nesting hole or a bee hive. Although diagnosis of the tree is mostly visual, specialized tools like wood augers may be used to take a core sample of the trunk.

Once the tree has been thoroughly evaluated, it is ranked numerically. A low score indicates that the tree is not hazardous, while a high score means that corrective measures should be undertaken.

So what is the best course of action if an arborist deems your tree to be hazardous? Abatement strategies can range from removal of a precarious limb to sawing the tree down. But what if you choose to forego a professional assessment and try to tackle the problem yourself? My advice is to leave the really large trees to the professionals who have the skills and specialized tools required to deal with your tree safely. However, you may want to try some restoration techniques on your smaller trees.

If you don't already have them, consider buying a few high-quality pruning tools. A pruning saw, which is curved to fit into the awkward tight areas of a tree's canopy, is a must. Secateurs, otherwise known as bypass pruners, are essential for removal of branches up to about one-half inch in diameter. Good secateurs will cost in the neighbourhood of $50, but are well worth it. Cheap secateurs are practically biodegradable. The one other tool that is well worth the investment is a pole pruner. It's essentially a glorified secateur placed on the end of a telescoping handle, and it's capable of removing branches from as high as twenty feet up into the canopy. Believe me, when you use a pole pruner for the first time, you'll feel like you've died and gone to heaven. The less time you spend perched precariously on a ladder, the better.

Before you attempt your first cut, it is imperative that you understand the basic principles of pruning. A well-illustrated, step-by-step instruction book is your best bet, along with some good advice from an experienced professional. But recognizing the fact that most of us cut first and query second, here are some tips to get you by.

Never flush cut a branch if at all possible. In other words, a short branch collar should remain close to the trunk, but don't cut right up to the trunk. Neither flush cuts nor long stubs heal properly, and both provide easy access for insects and diseases.

And forget the pruning paint. Paint of any type, according to the latest research, inhibits healing rather than promoring it. It was probably originally used to satisfy our human need to seal wounds—perhaps a little anthropomorphism, dare I say.

Always cut large branches three times. Start with a shallow, one half-inch-deep cut on the underside of the limb (known as an undercut) about a foot away from the trunk. Follow this initial cut with one a few inches to the outside of the undercut—but this time, cut completely through the branch, from top to bottom. (The reason for the undercut is to prevent the branch from stripping a large chunk of bark from the trunk as it falls.) For the final cut, remove the stub that remains, leaving just the short branch collar mentioned above.

Large limbs that are suspect structurally can be cabled. Cabling involves using hooks and steel cables to secure a weak limb to a strong one or to the trunk. It's not a good idea to use this technique on badly weakened limbs or those that could fall on, say, a car or garage. Although removal of the limb may be disheartening, safety is paramount.

Whether you hire a certified arborist to care for your tree or you choose to go it alone, just remember the two main objectives: the restoration of the tree's health and the preservation of yours.

—— BEST ADVICE——
for growing great hanging baskets...
Lots of fertilizer • Top quality potting mix • Big basket

WHILE DINING AT ONE OF MY FAVOURITE ITALIAN RESTAURANTS, I COULDN'T
HELP BUT NOTICE THAT THEIR HANGING BASKETS OF CALIBRACHOA WERE
BAKING AS THEY GENTLY SWAYED OVER THE PATIO. THESE PLANTS WERE SO
DRIED OUT THAT THEY WERE IN DANGER OF BECOMING WITHERED HUSKS.
SO WHAT DID I DO? WELL, I BORROWED A WATER JUG AND GAVE EACH
AND EVERY ONE OF THOSE BASKETS A GOOD SOAKING. I'D SEEN THIS
TERRIBLE NEGLECT AT OTHER RESTAURANTS, WHICH MADE ME THINK
THAT PERHAPS PEOPLE NEED TO KNOW JUST HOW MUCH CARE AND
ATTENTION HANGING BASKETS REQUIRE. "HANG IN THERE" IS MY
PRESCRIPTION FOR LUSH AND HEALTHY HANGING PLANTERS.

Hang In There

✻ ORIGINALLY PUBLISHED MAY 23, 1998 ✻

I love the look of a hanging basket dripping with flowers. Hanging baskets can be home to a dynamite show of foliage or a heavy yield of vegetables, but you've got to plan carefully for success.

First, choose the right container. I never put plants in anything smaller than a ten-inch pot; in fact, I prefer to use a twelve-inch pot whenever possible. Containers smaller than ten inches simply don't have enough soil volume to support the extensive root systems of the plants. Plant roots quickly fill all of the porous areas in small containers, occupying the very spaces where precious water and oxygen are meant to reside. If I were to water a plant in an eight-inch hanging basket before I headed to work—say, at 7:30 am—by the time I got back home, at 5:30 pm or so, the poor thing would be completely dried out. Lack of water is the number-one cause of poor performance in hanging baskets; in my experience, 90% of basket failures are due to insufficient moisture. One day of this harsh treatment probably won't kill the plant, but a few weeks of it sure will: plants stressed in this manner are more vulnerable to insect damage and disease. Surprisingly, a twelve-inch pot has nearly double the volume of a ten-incher, giving plants ample root space and providing a reservoir for water. Given that, the choice between them is clear.

Next, choose the right planting medium. Soil is something that professional growers spend a good deal of time examining, with good reason. After all, a large hanging basket has, let's say, six plants; a moss-lined wire basket may have thirty. The only reservoir of water and nutrients that the plant has access to is whatever the soil can yield. Soil properties are extremely important under these conditions. For containers, I always use a soilless mixture and never garden soil. Garden soil invariably becomes too compacted and heavy, and it often contains weeds and bugs.

Determining which soilless mixture is just right for a basket can be a challenge, but exciting new types continue to pop up. This year, we had the opportunity to try a new, promising soil and to help in the recycling process. The Alberta Newsprint Company (ANC) generates a lot of waste pulp as a byproduct of the paper-making process. This leftover pulp was initially thought of as waste and sent to the landfill—until now. ANC, with the assistance of the Alberta Research Council, has been experimenting with various bacteria that break pulp down into a product suitable for growing plants. The results have been excellent. Not only does this medium retain moisture exceptionally well, but the elevated ammonium levels cause vigorous deep-green leaf growth. A representative from ANC came out to monitor our progress a little over a week ago and was thrilled with the results. He told us that many recycling projects can reclaim only 5 to 10 % of waste material, but that this project has the potential to recycle 100% of ANC's leftover pulp. Naturally, we are very excited about this development.

Whichever soil you choose, keep to a regular, daily watering routine. When you're watering, add a pinch of 20-20-20 fertilizer to the can; plants in hanging baskets need those extra nutrients.

Now that we've dug into the soil question, here are a few plants that are very well suited to hanging baskets. My first recommendation is the scaevola, a plant with an interesting history. It's named after the Roman hero Mucius Scaevola, who, to prove his bravery, burned his hand off. I'm not sure if this is bravery or stupidity, but in any case, the plant that bears his name sports blue, fanlike flowers which are, indeed, roughly hand shaped. Appropriately enough, scaevola loves the heat. In fact, it can tolerate spells of 38°C; it's also able to resist temperatures as low as -2°C. Even though the scaevola is tough, don't let it wilt under any circumstances: loving the heat doesn't mean that it loves to be dry. Letting it wilt even once will result in reduced flower quality.

The new 'Wave' petunias have certainly caused some excitement here at the greenhouse. They're vegetatively propagated plants with lots of colour. The purple Wave can trail down at least four feet from the brim of the basket, and sometimes even five or six feet under optimum conditions. The pink Wave spreads a little less than the purple, but it's still a lovely flower. Both Waves can stand temperatures down to -4°C, so you'll enjoy them well into the fall. These petunias are heavy feeders, though, so be sure to add some extra fertilizer; feed them about twice as heavily as you would an average plant.

Another new arrival is the Million Bells, a variety of the genus *Calibrachoa* that resembles a miniature petunia with hundreds of small flowers. The flowers have yellow centres with pink, blue, or (forthcoming) white borders; its trailing growth habit looks great in a basket. Developed by Japanese plant breeders in 1988, this gorgeous creation is only now becoming available in North America. People are absolutely raving about this beauty; in fact, we've already sold out our stock of Million Bells! You may be able to find some even now, but it won't be easy. My advice for next year: get down to your garden centre early if you want to get your hands on this plant.

I've always liked lantanas in hanging baskets, but unfortunately, the old varieties were somewhat woody and sparse. Not so the new Patriot variety. These full, lush plants, smothered in yellow flowers, are much healthier and more vigorous than older lantanas. They love the heat and can withstand a period of drying out, although I still recommend keeping them watered regularly.

Torenias—also called the "wishbone flower" because their stamens are fused into a wishbone shape—are relatively uncommon in Canadian gardens, but there's no reason they should be. Another trailing plant, the torenia has lots of delicate baby-blue flowers that really catch the eye. It's easy to care for: just keep it moist and in a semi-shaded spot, and you'll enjoy the torenia's splendour for weeks. It will last right up until the first fall frost.

'Grandiflora' and 'Radiance' are two new portulaca varieties that are great for hot, dry locations. These forgiving plants are well adapted to dry environments and will spring back to life if you water them after they've dried out. Both also have big blooms: the Grandiflora's are rose coloured, while the Radiance sports rose and white bicoloured flowers. They're light feeders, too.

If you have a practical bent, you might want to try growing Tumbler tomatoes in your basket. I know I've talked about Tumblers before, but at the risk of driving people a little crazy, I'll say it again: this is the best basket tomato ever. It produces huge yields of absolutely scrumptious tomatoes. It's not uncommon to produce 300 fruit—each about double the size of a typical cherry tomato—from a single plant! It is a heavy feeder, though, so fertilize it heavily with 15-15-30 every time you water; this fertilizer has more potash, which is great for fruit quality. Alternatively, you can use a slow-release fertilizer like Nutricote. Just put three or four tablespoons in the pot once a month.

These are just a few of the possibilities for hanging baskets. Don't be afraid to experiment! I've had friends who have grown everything from cacti to carrots in hanging baskets, with great success. And if at first you don't succeed...well, try, try again. Just hang in there.

ONE OF THE BEST THINGS ABOUT GARDENING IS GETTING TO SHARE EXPERI-
ENCES WITH OTHER GARDENERS. OVER THE YEARS I'VE COLLECTED QUITE A
FEW STRANGE AND WONDERFUL TALES, AND I FELT THAT MY READERS WOULD
ENJOY THEM, TOO. HERE ARE A FEW OF THE QUIRKY BUT INNOVATIVE
GARDENING TRICKS THAT CONTINUE TO TICKLE MY FANCY TO THIS DAY.

Gardening on the Fringe

✺ ORIGINALLY PUBLISHED APRIL 3, 1999 ✺

Everyone has quirks, gardeners included. One of mine is a com-
pulsion to sow very thickly, a habit that probably has its roots in
crop failures that occurred early in my career. Even now, I keep a
watchful eye on my husband whenever he helps sow the vegetable
patch.

"Seed thicker, Ted! Seed thicker!" I cry. "It won't grow in the
package!"

"All right, dear, all right," he says, indulging my obsession.

Ted might tease me about my seeding philosophy, but he can't
deny that it usually results in high yields. Many gardeners have similar eccentricities—mad methods with unexpected payoffs. So before
you get into your garden this year, you might find some inspiration
in these unusual and interesting gardening vignettes, beginning with
a telephone conversation my son Jim fielded last summer.

"I need some help," the caller said. "My husband goes outside and pees on the potato patch every night."

"Oh, really?" Jim said.

"Will my potatoes be safe to eat?"

At first Jim thought that someone was pulling his leg, but eventually he figured out that the woman was serious. So he told her that as long as her husband wasn't peeing on the leaves (urine from any animal—husbands included—is bad for foliage), the potatoes would be fine.

On further reflection, the man's nightly "watering" ritual isn't completely nutty. Urine does contain small amounts of nitrogen—good for growth—and plants can always use more moisture. Besides, think of the many gallons of water saved by reduced flushing. Crackpot or ecologically conscious innovator? You be the judge.

On a more serious note, gardeners have come up with all kinds of innovative ways to enjoy gardening. Grafting, for example, is a fairly common practice, but grafting 20 varieties of apple onto a single tree? It's been done, by a fellow who visits our greenhouse regularly. Green apples, red apples, crabapples, early and late varieties...they all exist, side by side, on one tree. He exchanges cuttings with his neighbours, eager to increase the splendour and diversity of his amazing apple tree. It's really a wonder to behold.

The "potomato" is another remarkable grafting innovation. Potatoes and tomatoes are from the same botanical family, which means that they can be grafted together. The result is a plant with delicious tuberous roots down below and succulent fruit on top. Two plants, grown in the space of one! One lady I know grafts Early Girl tomatoes to Norland potatoes. Though I haven't tried this combination myself, she says the potatoes are the creamiest and the tomatoes the juiciest she's ever tasted. (It should be noted that there is some concern that poisonous solanin gets concentrated in tomato fruit in grafts of this type. My friend has been eating potomatoes for years with no ill effects, but anyone considering trying them should be aware of this concern. Fortunately, solanin is quite bitter, so fruit that has elevated levels of this substance won't taste very good.)

The standard, ungrafted tomato is Canada's most popular garden vegetable, so it's no wonder that people are always looking for new ways to help them grow bigger and stronger. Lloyd Patriquin of Edmonton created a "Tomato Cart" to give his tomato plants mobility. He grows his tomatoes in containers, keeps the containers in the cart, and moves the cart so that his plants are always in the sunniest spot in the yard. Plus, if frost looms, he simply pulls the cart into the warmth and safety of the garage for the night.

Another tomato lover I've encountered placed fallen crabapples from her tree in the tomato patch, claiming that it helped the tomatoes ripen faster. While I haven't witnessed it myself, there could be some basis in fact in this practice: crabapples give off ethylene gas, which has been shown to speed ripening in other fruits. Several of my friends toss eggshells or even Tums into their tomato patches, to add calcium to the soil. Others add Epsom salts to the garden: Epsom salts contain magnesium and sulphur, two essential elements for plant growth.

Here's one last tomato tip. Red, reflective plastic mulch, placed around the base of tomato plants, can spur their growth. Sunlight hits the mulch, and a good portion is converted to red light, which tomatoes love.

Finally, I've collected a number of miscellaneous insider tricks from friends and customers.

Rose lovers often add bananas to their gardens to add potassium to the soil. Roses do love potassium, and the high levels of this element present in bananas could certainly help to enrich the soil.

One of the most nefarious garden pests is the aphid. Tinfoil keeps aphids away—they don't like the intense reflected sunlight. Pie plates or strips of foil suspended in the air near your plants can really cut down on aphid problems. (Of course, the foil could be considered an eyesore.)

If you want a slightly bizarre look for your garden, why not try planting in some old shoes? One of our customers routinely rummages through her family's old footwear and fills hiking boots, rubbers, high-heeled pumps, and any other shoe she finds with flowers. I think this must be a "shoe-in" for the most unusual landscape design I've ever come across—although the "flower-beds" (flowers planted in old beds) I've seen here and there come close.

My favourite bit of garden advice is "live dangerously!" You never know—the crazy idea you have today might be the hottest horticultural tip of tomorrow!

——— BEST ADVICE ———
on buying new roses...
Buy container-grown • Bigger is better • Choose healthy, vigorous plants

WHEN NURSERY MANAGER SHANE NEUFELD DISCOVERED PAVEMENT ROSES, HE WAS ECSTATIC. MY HUSBAND TED, ON THE OTHER HAND, WAS LESS THAN IMPRESSED. "PAVEMENT ROSES? WHAT A TERRIBLE NAME!" NAMES ASIDE, PAVEMENT ROSES WERE AN INNOVATION IN ROSE GARDENING SO THRILLING THAT I HAD TO PASS THE DEVELOPMENT ALONG TO *Globe* READERS. RAISED TO THRIVE IN TRYING CONDITIONS, PAVEMENT ROSES ARE A TESTAMENT TO BOTH THE TENACITY OF PLANTS AND THE INGENUITY OF BREEDERS.

Pavement Roses Are Tough and Beautiful

⚘ ORIGINALLY PUBLISHED JANUARY 3, 1998 ⚘

You could describe pavements as solid, sturdy, and resilient—but beautiful? Well, that depends on the type of pavement to which you are referring.

The latest series of hardy shrub roses, which take the unusual name of 'Pavement' roses, are truly beautiful. Pavement roses are as lovely as any type of rose but are also remarkably tough. The name Pavement refers to the plant's suitability for street-side plantings. Pavements are tolerant of heat, drought, and cold, grow well in intense sunlight or partial shade, and tolerate high levels of road salt in the soil. Now, if a rose can take all that and still bloom beautifully, imagine how well it will do in the relative comfort of your own garden!

Pavement roses are generally low, sprawling bushes about 2.5 feet (75 cm) tall and 3 to 4 feet (90 to 120 cm) wide and are very attractive as groundcovers or as feature shrubs. There are eight varieties in the series, most of which have fragrant blooms all summer.

'Purple Pavement' has unusual, very attractive, semi-double, purplish red flowers offset by a yellow centre and borne on small trusses. If you prefer red roses, choose 'Scarlet Pavement' with its semi-double flowers and showy, bright-red rosehips.

In white, there are two choices: 'Snow Pavement', which has double flowers with a pink tint, and 'Pristine Pavement', which blooms pure white with perfumed semi-double roses.

Gardeners who prefer pink roses have the greatest selection. 'Showy Pavement' is superb with large pink flowers on arching branches. It blooms in wave after wave all summer. 'Foxi Pavement' has deep-pink, strongly scented, single flowers and attractive, deep-red rosehips. Both 'Pierrette Pavement' and 'Dwarf Pavement' bloom with dark-pink, semi-double flowers, but the dwarf version is a more compact bush.

Container-grown roses can be planted at anytime from early spring until a few weeks before the ground freezes in fall. Most roses do best in full sun, but Pavement roses also do fine in gardens with afternoon shade. Choose a site with well-drained soil, and work a generous handful of bonemeal into the soil of each hole before planting. Dig the planting hole wide enough for the entire root system to be laid out. The planting depth in the garden should be the same as it was in the pot.

Water roses regularly: they need more moisture than most plants. On average, water once a week to a depth of 1.5 inches (4 cm) and fertilize with 28-14-14 once a month in June, July, and August. Do not fertilize after August, to allow the plants time to prepare for winter.

In late fall, water the Pavement roses thoroughly shortly before the ground freezes—usually late October or early November. In the spring, wait until leaf buds appear and prune off any dead or broken branch tips just above the highest healthy bud. These relatively simple steps will keep your Pavement roses blooming profusely for years to come.

——— BEST ADVICE———
on meeting the challenge of the elements...
Consider the location • Start with lots of varieties • Be creative

SOMETIMES IGNORANCE IS AN ADVANTAGE. THAT WAS CERTAINLY THE CASE
WITH THE DUKOBOR FAMILIES IN MY HOMETOWN OF BUCHANAN,
SASKATCHEWAN. THEY ATTEMPTED TO GROW WATERMELONS AND
CANTALOUPE IN AN AREA WITH A REMARKABLY SHORT GROWING SEASON;
THEY COMPENSATED BY USING HOT BEDS TO INCREASE THE WARMTH
OF THE SOIL. THE FRUITS WERE SMALL, BUT VERY SWEET. "WE DIDN'T
KNOW YOU CAN'T GROW THAT HERE," WAS ONE RESPONSE TO ANOTHER
FARMER'S SURPRISE AT THEIR SUCCESS. CONVERSELY, I REMEMBER A
CUSTOMER WHO WOULDN'T BUY A POPLAR ONCE BILL TOLD HIM THAT
EVEN THESE NATIVE TREES ARE NOT 100% HARDY. STATISTICALLY SPEAKING,
WE GET A COLD SNAP SEVERE ENOUGH TO KILL POPLAR ONCE EVERY 30 YEARS
OR SO. THIS ARTICLE WAS WRITTEN TO EXPRESS THE CHOICE ALL
CANADIAN GARDENERS FACE: WHETHER TO SUBMIT TO OUR CLIMATE OR
RESIST IT. IT TURNS OUT THERE'S PLENTY OF ROOM FOR BOTH PHILOSOPHIES.

Two Paths

꙰ ORIGINALLY PUBLISHED MAY 15, 1999 ꙰

Two old sayings run "I'd rather fight than switch" and "A wise
man will bend with the wind rather than attempt to stand against
it." Each of these two contrary philosophies can be applied to the
garden. Every gardener must, at some point, make a choice: do I
attempt to change the environment so that I can grow coffee or figs in

Canada, or do I seek out plants that are ideally suited to my climate?

Those of us with stubborn dispositions are inclined to follow the first credo. I know a lady who is passionate about okra. Store-bought won't do; she has to grow the okra in her own garden. But okra is a heat-loving crop, one that I gave up growing years ago. It needs full sun all day long, warm nights, and a long growing season if it is to provide any fruit. Undaunted, this lady grows okra every year, seeing a crop through each season by sheer force of will. There hasn't been a year yet that she hasn't managed to raise at least a few fruits to maturity.

When she asked me how to improve her crop, I recalled what the farmers in my hometown of Buchanan, Saskatchewan used to do when I was a girl. They used manure to warm the soil for hot-season crops like peppers and squash. The breakdown of the manure added a surprising amount of heat to the soil—just stick your hand into an active compost pile and you'll see what I mean.

Today, there are more advanced ways to warm up crops. Row covers are one high-tech solution: they're lightweight, durable poly-ester sheets that shield rows of plants against wind and light frosts. They also capture warmth. The covers are porous to water, light, and air, so they can be left in place all day. They are particularly well suited for use in regions with cool nights. Hot caps and clear plas-tic shells can be placed over individual heat-loving plants; they in-crease the plants' temperature during the day and insulate them from frost at night, providing a towel or sheet is thrown over the covers. The "Wall of Water" is another alternative. It's a water-filled plastic container that surrounds the plant. The heat absorbed by the water during the day is released to the plants at night, effectively insulating them. It's not unusual for the night tem-perature around the plants to be increased by as much as 4 or 5°C. The caps, shells, and water walls can be used until early June, when the plants outgrow these containers. The polyester sheets can be effective for much longer as warm nighttime blankets for heat-loving plants.

Once summer arrives, fear of cold yields to fear of heat. Pansies in particular like temperatures in the mid teens to low twenties, and they abhor weather in the thirties. If you'd rather fight than switch, avoid planting pansies on a south- or west-facing wall, unless they are partially shaded by trees or other obstacles at the hottest time of day. Alternatively, plant the new, heat-tolerant pansy varieties like 'Bingo,' 'Crystal Bowl,' or 'Maxim.'

Canada is one of the best places in the world to grow strawberries–

they like it cool, too. But since our summers can be as extreme as our winters, strawberries often need a little human intervention to fight off the weather. Hot weather can damage the pollen on strawberry flowers, as well as overheat and damage the fruit. If the temperature in your garden rises above 30°C, reduce the heat by misting the strawberries with cool water to prevent the fruit from becoming malformed. (Of course, avoid late-evening misting or watering; otherwise, the fruit may be overwhelmed with mould.)

Although I'll do what I can to subvert Mother Nature in the cause of growing an out-of-zone plant, I'm a pacifist at heart, and sometimes it makes more sense to submit to her whims. For example, gardeners in areas with bright, sunny days and cool nights are often frustrated by their inability to grow certain plants. Rather than rage against the weather, many intrepid souls are switching tactics and trying out something new. The emerging popularity of alpine perennials is a prime example of this phenomenon. Alpines are well adapted to freezing temperatures, which makes them the perfect plant for a country where a frost can strike any day of the year. Calgarians have taken alpines into their hearts as well as their gardens. A strong alpine society has sprung up there, and no wonder: alpines are ideally suited to Calgary's high altitude.

If it's cool and rainy somewhere in Canada during midsummer, there's bound to be a heat wave somewhere else. Putting a few heat-loving plants in the garden is a good way to insure that you'll enjoy some colour no matter how hot it gets. Many of the super heat-tolerant plants are simply gorgeous. Scaevola, portulaca, and cacti all present a spectacular show when they're in full bloom. In the Alberta Badlands, prickly pear cacti decorate the sun-blasted valleys, their forbidding spines offset by delicate, colourful blooms. Indeed, prickly pears thrive from southern Alberta all the way up to the Peace River country - they, at least, are tough enough to endure the vagaries of Canada's climate.

I know a woman just a little way down the road who grows nothing but cacti and other succulents in her terraced, south-sloping backyard. She struggled for years with thirsty, high-maintenance plants before shifting her strategy and enjoying her beautiful (if prickly) low-maintenance garden. It's really a spectacular sight - dozens of blooming cacti sprawled across the yard in a shower of colour.

We are not completely helpless in the face of the elements, nor are we clever enough to foil them all of the time. Have the courage to change the things you can and the wisdom to accept—and adapt to—the things you cannot. Your garden will reward you for it.

―――― BEST ADVICE ――――
on growing a big tomato...
Get large-fruiting varieties • Cluster prune • Provide lots of TLC

MY SON JIM HAS HELPED ME OUT ALL ALONG IN THE CREATION
OF THESE COLUMNS, BUT HIS INFLUENCE REALLY SHINES THROUGH
IN THIS ARTICLE. I FELT I NEEDED A MALE PERSPECTIVE TO CATCH
THE ESSENCE OF WHY SOME PEOPLE GET A KICK OUT OF GROWING
THE BIGGEST TOMATO ON THE BLOCK. JIM'S SCIENTIFIC BACKGROUND
CAME IN HANDY TOO, PROVIDING ME (AND MY READERS) WITH PLENTY
OF PRACTICAL TIPS ON HOW TO GROW TRULY HUGE TOMATOES.

Huge Tomatoes

ↄ* ORIGINALLY PUBLISHED MAY 3, 1997 *ↄ

For most people, the backyard garden is a sanctuary, an island of tranquillity where they can relax after a tough day. For others, particularly men, it's a competitive arena where superlatives reign supreme, and the one plant that is incomparable for inciting competitiveness is the tomato—especially tomatoes that produce massive fruit.

Some gardeners with moderately elevated levels of testosterone are satisfied to simply grow the biggest tomatoes on the block, while others, like Gordon Graham of Edmond, Oklahoma, aren't satisfied until they've set the world record. Back in 1986, Mr. Graham won a place for himself in the Guinness Book of Records when he grew an astounding 3.5-kg tomato, which is just about the size of your average newborn human.

So exactly how do you get into the game?

The first, and obviously the most critical, step is to choose tomato plants that are genetically predisposed to producing large fruit. Some of the largest-fruiting cultivars available are 'Big Beef,' 'Big Boy,' 'Whopper' (which has recently been renamed OG50 in honour of *Organic Gardening* magazine's 50th anniversary), and of course 'Delicious,' the one that earned Gordon Graham his world record.

Rich, deep soil is absolutely essential for growing large fruit, but keep in mind that *soil* is just a catch-all term for "where the roots grow." The best growers use all sorts of composted material that may or may not include kitchen scraps, peat moss, leaves, loam vermiculite, and well-rotted manure. Choosing the best blend is a matter of personal preference, but the key words again are rich and deep. Tomatoes will easily root to a depth of 6 to 10 feet given the opportunity, and the greater the fibrous network of roots, the greater the fruit size. If, however, you prefer to grow tomatoes in containers, you're not out of the race. Just ensure that the containers have a volume of at least 22 litres. Smaller containers will yield nice tomatoes but are rather limited for growing colossal fruit.

While the soil must be rich and deep, it must also be consistently moist. Large-fruited varieties are particularly prone to fluctuating moisture and respond by turning black on the basal portion of the fruit. In humid areas of Canada, like the southern regions of Manitoba, Ontario, Quebec, and some parts of the Maritimes, tomatoes use on average just under 0.5 cm of water per day, while in the drier regions of the country, particularly the prairies, water consumption is just over 0.5 cm per day.

Containerized tomatoes require, proportionately, much higher quantities of water since their roots are confined to a finite space.

One surefire, but rather costly, way to ensure that your tomatoes are never thirsty is to install an irrigation system that consists of pipe, drip emitters, and a programmable timer that meters water to the tomatoes up to four times per day. This system costs about $100 but hey, are you in the game or not?

Even with rich, deep compost and lots of water, all tomato-growing champions supplement their soil with fertilizer. There is a lengthy list of fertilizers that will contribute to the growth of large fruit, ranging from the organic fertilizers like bonemeal, kelp, and fish to the so-called non-organic fertilizers like 20-20-20 and 15-15-30. Either type works very well, but there are a few basic principles of fertilizing to adhere to for the best plant growth. First, avoid heavy applications of nitrogen (the first number on the label); otherwise, the plants become excessively leafy and produce few flowers. Apply lots of phosphate (the second number on the label) when the plants are young to encourage vigorous rooting, and apply lots of potassium (the last number on the label) after fruit set to ensure high-quality fruit.

The optimum temperatures for tomatoes are quite easy to remember but somewhat difficult to achieve consistently. If the daytime temperatures are a constant 27°C and the nighttime temperature around 17°C for most of the growing season, tomato plants grow exceedingly well. Not surprisingly, the largest commercial tomato farms are located in the extreme southern portion of Ontario, where average summer temperatures closely parallel these values.

But if you live in regions of Canada where temperatures are less than ideal for tomatoes, simply choosing a warm southwest spot near the house will help enormously. In regions where nighttime temperatures frequently dip into the single digits, lightweight insulating fabrics can be draped over the tomatoes at night to reduce heat loss.

Sunlight is the engine that drives plant growth, and for tomatoes, the more unobstructed sunlight they receive from morning until evening, the better. Not surprisingly, the long summer days common to the northern regions offset, to a certain degree, a cooler growing season. Shade is the bane of tomatoes, and sunlight is free, so choose your site wisely.

Pollination is an often-neglected aspect of successful tomato fruit growth, perhaps because tomatoes seem to get along just fine without any human intervention. This statement is partially true, since tomatoes are almost entirely self-pollinated. However, flowers that are helped along tend to produce bigger, smoother fruit. Pollinating tomato flowers is simple. It involves tapping each flower cluster or truss with your finger. Better yet, vibrate each truss with an old electric toothbrush. Whichever method is used, hand pollination should be undertaken when the flowers are most receptive, which is between mid-morning and mid-afternoon, on bright, sunny days.

The final, and most difficult, task is to cluster-prune. This is a particularly sad event because it involves choosing the most promising fruit on a cluster and then disposing of 4 or 5 perfectly healthy fruit. This is the only way to have at least a fighting chance of growing a 3.5-kg monster. After all, you have to ask yourself: are you in the game or not?

——— BEST ADVICE ———
as your garden matures…
Adapt to change • Plan ahead • Don't be afraid to start again

NO GARDEN IS ETERNAL AND UNCHANGING. AS THE SEASONS PASS, SO DO THE ENVIRONMENTAL CONDITIONS IN THE GARDEN. I WAS INSPIRED TO WRITE THIS ARTICLE BY THE PLIGHT OF MY FRIENDS THE IRWINS, WHOSE GRASS WAS GRADUALLY DYING OFF BECAUSE THE GROWING TREES WERE SHADING OUT MORE AND MORE LIGHT. THEY WOUND UP RIPPING UP THE GRASS AND REPLACING IT WITH A PATCH OF SHADE-TOLERANT PANSIES. WHEN ANOTHER FRIEND REPORTED A SIMILAR PROBLEM WITH HER TOMATOES, I KNEW THAT IT WAS AN ISSUE I NEEDED TO ADDRESS.

Seasons in the Sun

❧ ORIGINALLY PUBLISHED JULY 4, 1998 ❧

A friend of mine had always grown wonderful tomatoes in her backyard. She loved their fresh taste and the satisfaction she got from growing the plants herself. Over the years, however, she noticed that the flavour of her tomatoes gradually began to diminish. She hadn't changed her watering or fertilizing practices, and she was planting the same varieties year after year, so the reason for the change was elusive.

My friend also had several trees in her backyard. She finally noticed that as her trees grew, they were shading out the tomato patch. The tomatoes were being deprived of their crucial source of energy—the sun's rays—and that was enough to rob the tomatoes of their flavour. Such stories remind me that the sun has the most profound influence in the garden. Success in the garden ultimately revolves around the sun.

Just out of curiosity, I pulled out my copy of *Climates of Canada* to see how summer sunlight levels vary across the country, since day length is one of the ways that the sun affects plant growth. Many people are surprised to learn that corn will grow in Yellowknife, despite its rather short growing season. This is possible because northern areas have many more hours per day of sunlight, which somewhat offsets the cooler temperatures in these regions. Although the average frost-free period in Yellowknife is only 111 days, on June 15 the sun rises at 2:45 am and sets at 10:30 pm! Compare the average hours of sunlight between Yellowknife and Toronto: the southern city receives a little over 1000 hours of sunlight during July, while Yellowknife gets almost 1400 hours of sun. It's no wonder that cabbages of monstrous size are often grown in the Territories, since those long days allow the leaves to use more sunlight, which generates more growth. The same sort of effect happens in Peace River, in northern Alberta: corn grown there will mature only a few days later than corn grown in Medicine Hat, close to the US border—even though the corn in Peace River gets planted much later! I have friends in both communities who grow vegetables, and it's interesting to watch the friendly competition between north and south: whose crops will mature first? The south usually wins, but it is by no means a foregone conclusion.

The same combination of long days and cool temperatures creates the most vibrant flower colours, too, and long days can boost flower production. Snapdragons, for example, often enjoy an increase in flower numbers as the day's length increases. Flower stalks that mature in June are about one-third longer than those that mature later in the season.

As you might suspect, low light levels tend to have adverse effects on nearly all plants. Fruit flavour can deteriorate quite noticeably under these conditions; tomatoes that get less than six hours of sunlight per day may taste mealy and unpleasant, and the sharp tang of apples won't develop without plenty of bright sunlight. Most flowering plants won't bloom at all if there isn't enough light. Mandevilla, for example, is a gorgeous vine that produces pink, trumpet-shaped flowers, but it needs to accumulate a lot of energy from the sun's rays before it will even consider producing flower buds.

However, too much sun can be just as bad as too little. Sunscald—the plant version of a sunburn—is a concern right across the country on hot, bright days. Plants affected by sunscald develop pale-yellow or greyish white patches on their leaves or fruit. This often happens when the plants are in a location that reflects the sun's rays, such as next to a white stucco wall. I've had the fruit of my pepper and tomato plants burned badly by reflected light, so I've learned to plant them where this won't happen; next to a darker-coloured wall, for example.

One danger, though, is exaggerated. According to a commonly held belief, you shouldn't water on really hot days because water droplets on the leaves will magnify the sun's rays and burn the plant. I can't tell you how many times I've heard this, from friends, professional growers' magazines, and even community-service bulletins. But think about it for a minute: we often get bursts of rain followed by intense sun. I've never noticed hundreds of holes or burn marks on my trees or on the grass. In all my years of watering, I've seen no evidence of water droplets searing leaves or fruit. Perhaps this notion came about because pouring cold water on plants like African violets can sometimes cause chilling injury. White spots appear on leaves and flowers because of the sudden cold shock, but sunlight is not to blame.

There's not much we can do about day length or the sun's intensity, of course, but we can breed varieties that are adapted to these conditions. Strawberries, for example, typically bear fruit in June, when the days are longest. There are everbearing varieties as well, which bear mostly in June, but also sporadically through the course of the summer. The newest varieties of strawberry are the day neutrals. These plants are not influenced by day length and so bear fruit heavily from July until the first frost. Day neutrals were developed by crossing and back-crossing June-bearing types with a wild everbearing strawberry found in the mountains of Utah. ("Back-crossing" is the process of crossing hybrid varieties with original, heirloom cultivars.) The result is a vigorous plant that bears fruit much longer and much less sporadically than other varieties. I switched to the 'Tri-Star' day-neutral variety several years ago, and the difference in yield and flavour has been just tremendous. I always look forward to seeing what kinds of new varieties will be tested in our trial gardens; many of these, like the day- neutral strawberries, will be able to make more efficient use of the sun's energy.

Keeping the sun in mind will give you a big leg up in your pursuit of the perfect garden. As the Beatles used to say...here comes the sun, and it's all right.

——— BEST ADVICE———
On dealing with pests...
Understand the bug • Avoid overkill • Plant extra

ORGANIC GARDENING HAD BEEN IN THE NEWS SO FREQUENTLY THAT I
DECIDED IT WAS TIME FOR ME TO WEIGH IN ON THIS COMPLEX AND OFTEN
EMOTIONAL ISSUE. THE DEBATE SHOWS NO SIGN OF ABATING. EACH DAY BRINGS
NEW INFORMATION TO LIGHT ON ORGANIC GARDENING, AND MY SON JIM
WROTE AN ENTIRELY DIFFERENT ARTICLE ON THE SUBJECT JUST A COUPLE OF
WEEKS BEFORE THIS BOOK WENT TO PRESS. IT LOOKS LIKE THERE WILL BE
SOMETHING TO TALK ABOUT IN THE FIELD OF ORGANIC GARDENING FOR QUITE
SOME TIME TO COME. HERE'S MY ORIGINAL TAKE ON THE SUBJECT, FOCUSSING
ON THE ISSUE OF ORGANIC AND CHEMICAL PESTICIDES.

Pesticides

☙ ORIGINALLY PUBLISHED JULY 25, 1998 ❧

I was speaking to a group of gardeners recently when one of
them asked me about switching from chemical pesticides to strictly
organic, natural controls. I thought for a moment and said, "Well, it's
a good idea in principle, but be prepared to eat a few bugs." Judging from the expressions on their faces, that probably wasn't the
answer the group wanted to hear. It was, however, the only honest
reply I could make.

Actually, I'm getting asked questions like this more and more
these days. These days, commercial growers often ask, "How are the
bios working?" Not too long ago, I would have been bewildered by

such a question. What are bios? Well, they're biological controls, a relatively new method of dealing with pests.

In the world of gardening, almost nothing is as controversial as pesticide. To spray or not to spray is the question these days, and the rise of organic gardening, including biological controls, seems to indicate that many gardeners are choosing to shy away from chemicals. But is pesticide use really the black-and-white issue it's made out to be?

I remember when DDT was thought of as the final solution to bug control—it was a common presence on many farms. I even remember using it back in the 1960s. But ever since DDT was shown to cause all kinds of ecological damage, all pesticides have been thought of as evil, environment-destroying, and dangerous to public health and safety. There's a lot of truth to this view, but it's not the whole truth. Of course DDT is dangerous. It doesn't break down but accumulates in animal fat as it moves up the food chain, quickly reaching lethal levels for many animals. It killed as many beneficial insects as pests, and has caused a good deal of human suffering. On the other hand, DDT is credited with saving millions of lives, in tropical areas like Africa and southeast Asia, since it devastated the malaria-carrying mosquito population in those regions.

As the saying goes, there are two sides to every story. DDT should have been checked much more thoroughly for potential problems. But thanks in part to the lesson of DDT, the world of chemical controls has changed. The public outrage over DDT has helped to ensure that pesticides being developed today are a far cry from the pesticides of old.

The biggest change in the way that pesticides work is that they have become much more pest-specific. In the old days, pesticides would kill indiscriminately; they wiped out everything, good and bad bugs alike. Today, pesticides go after one or two kinds of bad insects, while leaving many of the beneficial ones alone.

For example, we've had great success with a new commercial-use pesticide (or "biocide," as many of the new types are now called) here at the greenhouse. It's made up of nematodes, microscopic worms that work by tunneling into pests like fungus gnats and root maggots. While they are inside the pest, the nematodes release bacteria that kill the host insect. The nematodes will grow and reproduce inside the pest, eventually being released back into the soil. It may sound a little grisly, but it's very effective. Best of all, the nematodes won't hurt people, plants, or beneficial insects.

For evidence of how far alternatives to chemical pesticide have come, you don't have to look very far. Every year *The Farm Chemicals Handbook* arrives on my son Jim's desk. It is an annual publication for commercial growers that lists every pesticide in the world that's currently on the market. Jim tells me that at one time, the *Handbook* made no mention of biological controls; today, there are 50 pages devoted to the subject. Developers realize that the public is concerned about environmental damage, so they are coming up with an ever-growing list of products that are less damaging to our ecosystem than traditional chemical sprays. Here you'll find everything from *Aphidotetes aphidimyza*—a fly-like insect that attacks aphids—to Ladybug Lure, the trade name of a pheromone that draws these beneficial, pest-killing insects to your garden. Natural hormones to affect insects' mating behaviours and growth patterns, mechanical traps, ecologically safe bacteria…there are scores of ways to deal with pests while still keeping the environment in mind. Mention is even made of experimental anti-feeding compounds that induce insects to stop eating; they quickly starve to death.

From time to time I get samples of other biocontrols. The most recent gift was a bottle of wolf urine. After wrinkling my nose for a moment, I handed it over to Jim. He pointed out that it's actually a clever product: the urine is spread around the garden and the scent fools pests like deer and rabbits into believing that there are wolves nearby. This deters these larger pests from visiting your vegetable patch. My daughter-in-law Valerie is testing it now, and I'm eager to see how effective this product is. (I should point out that we've always used controls like fences or netting to protect our vegetable crops from wildlife; shooting or trapping them has never been our style.)

Developers can put all kinds of environmentally friendly products on the market, but the end-users—the growers, farmers, and home gardeners—have to help too. That's why I'm so glad that the philosophy of pesticide use has changed. These days, responsible growers won't saturate the area with pesticides at the first sign of pests; instead, they monitor their gardens or farms with sticky traps that serve to identify any pests and to estimate their numbers. After the level of infestation has been determined, growers have to decide if spraying is warranted. If the level of infestation is slight, spraying is generally avoided. This is quite a change in attitude; in the old days, the sight of a single bug could often set off a frenzy of spraying. If the infestation is large, then the best possible pesticide—that is, the one that targets the specific problem pest—is applied.

On our farm, pesticide was always a last resort. "One for me, one for the bugs," is what I used to say when I went out seeding. We usually had stands good enough to allow the bugs and larger animals to share in the bounty, but some years we just couldn't spare any of our crop; that's when we sprayed. We follow the same philosophy in our greenhouse today: don't jump the gun when using pesticides. Often, infestations will start with one or two plants in the garden hot-spots. The simplest solution, and the most common one at my greenhouse, is to just throw the infected plants into the compost pile rather than getting out the spray. (The heat of the decomposing matter kills the pests, so it's perfectly safe to use this compost in your garden.) Evaluate the level of danger to the plants and then decide if pesticides should be used.

Eventually, I think we will see pest controls that are 100% environmentally friendly without sacrificing effectiveness. Until that day arrives, the best we can do is to act responsibly by using the safest chemical and biological controls available, and only when absolutely necessary.

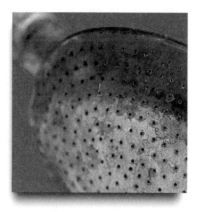

AS YOU WILL SEE WHEN YOU READ OF THIS ARTICLE, NOTHING DRIVES ME
CRAZIER THAN SEEING WATER BEING WASTED. THAT'S WHY THE DEVELOPMENT
OF A NEW DRIP-IRRIGATION SYSTEM GAVE ME SUCH PLEASURE–AT LAST, AN
EASY–TO–USE WATERING METHOD THAT WILL HELP PEOPLE CONSERVE THIS
PRECIOUS RESOURCE. I HOPE YOU'LL CONSIDER GIVING IT A TRY TOO!

A New Way to Irrigate

◢ ORIGINALLY PUBLISHED 17 JULY 1999 ◣

Few things irritate me more than the sight of precious water
pouring out of the tap and straight down the drain. A childhood
spent in a small, drought-prone Saskatchewan town taught me how
precious water is. Gardens in particular consume plenty of
water, especially during hot spells in July and August. Thankfully,
reducing our consumption is not difficult.

When people think of watering the flower or vegetable garden,
they usually picture water wands, hoses, watering cans, sprinklers, or
rain barrels. What doesn't immediately come to mind is drip irrigation. Drip irrigation is a very efficient method of distributing
water to plants—one drop at a time. This is not new technology, but
it is almost unknown to home gardeners; it is much more common
in large-scale operations. In our greenhouse, we use hundreds of

metres of drip tubes to irrigate crops like hanging baskets and geraniums. In California, thousands of kilometres of drip-irrigation tubing are used to water strawberry fields.

Drip-irrigation systems are simple, consisting of lengths of thin plastic pipe fitted with special emitters at regular intervals—every 30 cm or so. Each emitter is a tiny plastic labyrinth that slows water flow and equalizes it so that water drips out at the same rate along the length of the piping.

Drip irrigation saves water because the pipes are laid on the ground in rows close to the plants' root systems. The water has less opportunity to evaporate, since it is not being sprayed into the air and onto foliage, as is the case with overhead sprinklers. Not splashing water onto the foliage has one major side effect: the incidence of leaf diseases is greatly reduced. I remember ruining one string bean crop by aggressively irrigating it with overhead sprinklers. Almost overnight, all of the leaves were covered with bean blight, a rust-like disease properly referred to as *Xanthomonas phaseoli*. Sprinklers tend to splash mud laden with soil-borne diseases right onto the stems and leaves of plants. When the leaves are left dry and clean, fewer bacteria and fungi have the opportunity to become established.

With drip irrigation, patience is a virtue. Since the water is applied a drop at a time, irrigation is unspectacular and often seems interminable. But it does work, and well. As the water drips out of the emitters, it seeps into the soil vertically and horizontally. (Sandy soils have the least horizontal movement, while clay soils have the greatest.) Drip irrigation is best suited to plants that have been established for several weeks, rather than seedlings, since the root systems of many seedlings are too small to reach the moisture.

Drip-irrigation systems are relatively inexpensive and easy to use. The pipe is surprisingly lightweight. I've picked up a 150-m roll of pipe and I'm sure it didn't weigh any more than 5 kg. To illustrate just how simple this stuff is to use, imagine a vegetable garden with dimensions of 6 m by 6 m with 10 rows of vegetables. The drip is laid down along each row, so that there are 10 6-m lengths of tubing. At one end, all of the individual lengths of tubes are plugged or just folded over and clamped. At the other end, they are all connected together. Barbed plastic connectors are simply pushed into the tubing. No tools or clamps are required, and even someone who is severely mechanically challenged (like me) will have no problem hooking the pipe together. Connect the system to your outside tap, and voila, you're on your way to conserving hundreds of litres of water per year. One tip: before you begin, leave the coiled tube in the sun to heat up for a while to make it soft and pliable. Otherwise, it jumps around like an angry snake when you're trying to install it.

Drip tubing is especially convenient to lay down alongside rows of crops like carrots, onions, or corn, or even in beds of annuals and perennials, providing that it's installed early, before the plants have become too dense to allow tubing to slide in between. Dependable and relatively inexpensive water timers can be attached between the water faucet and the drip tubing to set the frequency of irrigation: once a day, once a week, twice a day, or whatever you prefer. Duration can be set as well: two minutes, ten minutes, and so forth. If you know what the flow rate is in litres per minute and what the water requirements of the crop are, you can calculate exactly how long you should leave the tubes on to meet the plants' needs. Removal in the fall is simple. Just pull it up, pull off the connectors, and store.

Of course, there will always be times when conventional watering will be more efficient than installing drip irrigation. If I use a hose to water, I always attach a water wand rather than one of those dreadful gun-like nozzles. Water wands deliver a focussed but gentle spray, and if you're careful and hold the wand close to the plants, little water is wasted. And of course, sometimes low-tech solutions are still effective. Water collected in rain barrels and distributed with a trusty watering can is still one of the best ways to irrigate your plants while also being a conservationist.

JIM STEPPED IN ONCE AGAIN TO GIVE ME A HAND WITH THIS ARTICLE. GOING
TO SCHOOL HELPS: IT WAS JIM'S UNIVERSITY TRAINING THAT GAVE US THE
CHANCE TO UNDERSTAND AND TAKE ADVANTAGE OF THE CONCEPT OF FIELD
HEAT, WHICH CAN HAVE SUCH A DRAMATIC IMPACT ON THE QUALITY OF
HARVESTED VEGETABLES. BEFORE JIM'S EXPERIENCES AT THE UNIVERSITY OF
ALBERTA, WE'D RUINED A HUGE CROP OF CARROTS BY PULLING THEM UP,
WASHING THEM, AND STORING THEM IN A COOLER–BEFORE TAKING STEPS TO
REMOVE THE FIELD HEAT. IF WE'D KNOWN THEN WHAT WE KNOW NOW, WE
COULD HAVE SAVED A WHOLE TON OF ROTTING VEGETABLES. AS WE FOUND
OUT, A BUCKET OF ICE WATER CAN BE YOUR BEST HARVESTING TOOL.

Garden Harvesting

ℐ ORIGINALLY PUBLISHED AUGUST 16, 1997 ℐ

In my vegetable and berry patch it is truly the best and worst of
times. With temperatures hovering in the low to mid thirties this
past week, the heat-loving vegetables like corn, cucumbers, and
squash are thriving, while the strawberries, lettuce, and spinach are
flagging considerably.

Harvesting can be tricky when it is so warm. It's something of a
challenge to get the produce from the patch to the table with all of
the subtle flavours and textures intact. One of the most common
mistakes that most of us make during harvesting is picking the crop

too late in its life cycle. Red tomatoes, for example, should always be picked at the pink stage of fruit development and then left on the kitchen counter to ripen. If the fruit is left on the vine until it is fully red, it has already begun to degrade, losing sweetness and flavour while acquiring a mealy texture.

The same principle applies to corn. Once the kernels have become deep yellow or orangey, many of the wonderful sugars have been converted to starch, and, in my opinion, the cobs are best reserved for livestock. One rule of thumb for the timing of the corn harvest is to wait about three weeks from the time that the silk fully emerges on the cob before you pick. At that time the corn is at its peak of perfection.

Some of the very fragile berries like strawberries and raspberries are even trickier to harvest, not because of the maturity question but rather because they are so darn delicate. Raspberries in particular are so soft that they can easily be crushed if stacked too deep. They should never be layered more than three berries deep. Of course, having enough baskets and considerable patience is essential.

Harvesting at just the right stage of maturity is critical for ensuring that most of the flavour and texture of the crop is preserved, but it's still only half the battle. Removing the "field heat" is the other half, and it's not as easy as one might think, especially when the weather is hot.

Sticking the vegetables or fruit in the refrigerator seems to be the obvious, simple solution for removing heat. Unfortunately, refrigerators are designed to keep cool things cool, not to remove heat from warm objects. As a result, it takes hours to cool the produce down to the temperature setting of the refrigerator.

The other problem is that refrigerators are usually set at the 5° to 8°C range, while most fruits and vegetables taste best when rapidly cooled down to within a degree or two of freezing. Refrigerators also possess desert-like humidity, and virtually all tender produce will lose moisture at an alarming rate if left exposed to the dry air for even a few hours.

The simplest and still the most effective way to cool produce is to plunge it into a tub or bucket of ice water for ten or twenty minutes and then put it in the refrigerator. The ice-bath treatment works extremely well for vegetables like corn, broccoli, cauliflower, and carrots, just to name a few. In fact, if corn doesn't take the plunge, it can become starchy in less than one hour if harvested when the weather is hot. That's why the old adage about taking the pot of boiling water to the corn patch rather than the corn to the pot is not too farfetched.

Strawberries, raspberries, and blackberries deteriorate so quickly in hot weather that at times it seems nearly impossible to get them to the table intact. The shelf life of raspberries, even when they are held at a temperature of about 10°C, is only one quarter of what it would be if held at 0°C. If the berries are picked when temperatures are in the thirties, they are often ruined within a few hours. The ice-bath treatment would remove the heat effectively from the berries, but, because they are so fragile, the cure would kill the patient.

I've had quite good success covering shallow baskets of fruit with plastic and leaving them in the ice water for half an hour prior to storing them in the fridge. Warm fruit placed directly in the fridge not only cools very slowly, but moist air condenses on the fruit, creating an ideal environment for fuzzy graymould.

If you really want to become a master harvester, it's best to develop a fondness for sunrise, because that's when the air is coolest and the vegetables and fruit contain the least heat field. The only caveat is that the fruit should be harvested once the dew has dried.

If you're not an early bird, take consolation in the fact that by late fall Mother Nature will undoubtedly solve any heat problems.

──── BEST ADVICE ────
on how to grow great corn...
Lots of nitrogen • Water heavily at tassel stage • Pick and eat within an hour

MY FAMILY IS A LITTLE SPOILED WHEN IT COMES TO CORN, HAVING ENJOYED IT FRESH FROM THE GARDEN FOR MANY YEARS NOW. OUR STAFF WRITER EARL WOODS WAS NEVER A BIG FAN OF CORN, BUT SHORTLY AFTER HE STARTED WORKING HERE, JIM TOOK HIM OUT INTO THE CORNFIELD AND TOLD HIM TO TRY OUT A COB OF JULY GEM. EARL WAS A LITTLE DUBIOUS. "WHAT, YOU WANT ME TO EAT IT RAW?" HE ASKED DOUBTFULLY. "GIVE IT A TRY," JIM SAID, AND EARL DID. "HEY, THIS IS REALLY GOOD!" HE EXCLAIMED, SURPRISED BY THE TASTE OF THE SWEET AND TENDER KERNELS. FRESHNESS AND VARIETY MAKE ALL THE DIFFERENCE IN THE QUALITY OF A CORNCOB. THERE'S A REASON WHY SOME CORN IS USED AS CATTLE FEED!

The Colonels of Corn

✤ ORIGINALLY PUBLISHED SEPTEMBER 6, 1997 ✤

Every year right around this time the mood around the kitchen table takes a subtle shift.

Most of the new corn varieties have finally matured, and lunch-time is devoted as much to criticizing as it is to enjoying the wonderful fresh taste of home-grown corn on the cob.

Evaluating exactly which varieties are the best is a task that is considerably more difficult than first meets the eye because sweet corn is not simply a vegetable consisting of a bunch of varieties.

Rather, it's a vegetable that can be divided into categories, each of which contains a bunch of varieties.

The traditional category of corn that many of us ate as children is called "normal" corn. Normal varieties are designated in seed catalogues by the symbol "SU," and one of the characteristics of SU corn is that the sugar in the kernel converts to starch rapidly, resulting in corn that becomes tasteless when it is even slightly overmature.

Some of the new varieties of normals can remain quite sweet a little longer than the traditional normals, and most have excellent germination in cold soils, but because of their inherent starchy flavour, I haven't grown any of them in years.

In my opinion, most of the improvement in sweet corn varieties has evolved from the breeding efforts within the "sugar-enhanced" or "SE" category. Sugar-enhanced varieties convert their sugar to starch at much the same rate as the normals, but because they have a higher sugar content to begin with, they remain sweeter much longer. Some sugar enhanced varieties are designated by the symbol "Se," meaning that only about 25% of their kernels have elevated sugar levels, which pretty much means that they play second fiddle to the SEs.

All of the SEs are not only very sweet but also very tender, which unfortunately makes them prone to damage from mishandling during long-distance shipping and vulnerable to mechanical harvesters. That's why you're more likely to see the SEs at farmers' markets rather than at large grocery stores.

Because the SE varieties are so wonderfully tender and sweet, they have earned the lion's share of space in my corn patch. The only drawback of the sugar-enhanced varieties is, reputedly, their poor germination in cold soil, which I have yet to witness, and I always sow in early May.

Having unabashedly stated my bias for the SE varieties, I cannot ignore what some people, including my grandchildren, feel is the best category of sweet corn: the supersweets. Supersweet varieties are symbolized as "SH," which alludes to the fact that the seed is conspicuously shrunken and wrinkled when dry.

The supersweet varieties are by far the sweetest of any types of corn. At maturity, they have the highest sugar content of all the corn categories, and they tend not to convert their sugar to starch readily. Even after they become severely overmature, they still remain remarkably sweet. The only criticism I have of the supersweets is that the sugar overwhelms the taste buds, concealing the more delicate corn flavours; the kernels can also be quite tough and chewy. One additional problem for home gardeners is that the supersweets must be isolated from the normal and sugar-enhanced varieties, otherwise cross-pollination will occur and the kernels on the supersweet cobs will acquire a bland, starchy flavour.

A recently introduced category of corn that is gaining in popularity is a bit of a curiosity. It's actually a blend of either normals and sugar-enhanced varieties or normals and supersweets. The cobs contain about 25% normal kernels, while the remainder are the sugar-enhanced or supersweet. The result is a blend of flavours that I suppose is designed to satisfy the tastes of all corn aficionados. However, much like the corn, my feelings are mixed on this conglomeration because although it is very pleasant to eat, it tries to be all things to all people and ultimately just doesn't quite make it.

Incidentally, if you're wondering why I haven't mentioned the now sacrosanct variety 'Peaches and Cream,' it's because Peaches and Cream no longer exists. Today, any corn variety that has a blend of white and yellow kernels is erroneously referred to as Peaches and Cream. In fact, all of the corn categories contain at least some bicoloured varieties. Bicolour corn is not necessarily better than solid yellows or solid whites, but it continues to gain in popularity.

Finally, the corn varieties that my family was most impressed with are Grant, an exceptionally early, solid yellow SE variety that I'm sure could be grown well into the Yukon and Northwest Territories; Speedy Sweet, a very sweet, early bicoloured SE variety that has remarkable flavour for such an early corn; Extra Early Supersweet, an extraordinarily sweet yellow SH variety that my grandchildren love; Sweet Rhythm, a new SESh, bicolour combination; and Merlin, a long-eared, yellow SE variety that has very tender kernels and excellent flavour, but requires too long a season for many regions in Canada.

———— BEST ADVICE ————
on growing great peppers...
Start early • Remember they love the heat • Lots of water & fertilizer

EVERY YEAR, JIM TRIES TO TRICK SOMEONE INTO EATING A SUPER-HOT PEPPER.
HE USUALLY DOES THIS BY POPPING A MILD PEPPER INTO HIS MOUTH, WAXING
ENTHUSIASTIC ABOUT ITS GREAT TASTE, AND THEN GIVING A SIMILAR-LOOKING
BUT FAR HOTTER VARIETY TO HIS VICTIM. JIM'S ANNUAL SHENANIGANS
REMINDED ME OF TED'S UNFORTUNATE ENCOUNTER WITH HOT PEPPERS,
AND I COULDN'T RESIST SHARING THE STORY WITH MY FELLOW CANADIANS.
NATURALLY, I TOOK PAINS TO ADD SOME USEFUL INFORMATION ABOUT
WHY HOT PEPPERS ARE HOT, IN THE HOPES THAT OTHER PEPPER
LOVERS COULD AVOID THE HOT SPOT TED FOUND HIMSELF IN.

Hot Peppers

⚜ ORIGINALLY PUBLISHED MAY 24, 1997 ⚜

If you can't take the heat, stay out of the washroom. At least,
that's the advice I should have given to my husband Ted once when
he was helping me chop up some extremely hot peppers for pick-
les. Having heard me complain bitterly about how the peppers were
burning the skin off my hands, he marched straight into the bath-
room and inexplicably failed to wash his hands before relieving
himself. The grim result was...well, let's just say the dancing and
grabbing that ensued would have done Michael Jackson proud.

What gives hot peppers their potent kick is a flavourless plant oil called capsaicin. The oil acts directly on the pain receptors beneath the skin, and as little as one drop of pure capsaicin in 100,000 drops of water can cause tongue blisters.

Three species of peppers are capable of producing capsaicin: *Capsicum annuum*, which includes the jalapeño as well as the mild bell pepper; *Capsicum frutescens*, more commonly called tabasco; and finally, the mother of all hot peppers, *Capsicum chinense*, which includes the habanero and Scotch bonnet.

And just how hot are these peppers? Wilbur L. Scoville, a scientist at Parke-Davis University in the United States, devised a scale to evaluate the capsaicin in peppers called, not surprisingly, the Scoville scale. When the peppers are ranked according to capsaicin content, jalapeños, cayennes, and habaneros show a rather remarkable range in potency.

Jalapeños, which taste plenty hot to me, are by Scoville standards rather tepid with a score of between 2500 and 5000. Cayennes are significantly hotter, with a fiery 30,000 to 50,000 units, while the habaneros and Scotch bonnet rocket to the top of the list with a flaming 300,000 Scoville units!

I've grown both the habanero and the Scotch bonnet, but I must confess that I have no idea how they taste. The culinary appeal of anything approaching the heat levels of these two peppers is virtually nil from my perspective, but they are interesting to grow. My son Jim, who is a little more adventurous, took a tiny bite of one small habanero fruit and described the sensation as "the same as swishing battery acid inside your mouth."

If you want to try growing habaneros, be aware that they require a long growing season. Habaneros are indigenous to the Caribbean (habanero means "from Havana"), so large, vigorous greenhouse-started plants are a must, especially in regions with short growing seasons.

All peppers, whether they are hot or mild, enjoy full sun and warm temperatures, particularly in early summer. Daytime temperatures anywhere from 22 to 30°C are ideal, while nighttime temperatures 14°C or higher will ensure good fruit set. Cool nights will inevitably cause the blossoms to drop before pollination can occur, resulting in huge, bushy pepper plants with very few fruit.

Peppers grow best in soil that is somewhat acidic (pH 5.5 to 6.5) and moist. Good soil fertility is critical for success, so I like to feed the plants once a week with 15-15-30 fertilizer. Peppers also need lots of calcium for healthy fruit and magnesium for vigorous leaves.

Since dolomitic lime contains both calcium and magnesium, it can be added to the soil during transplanting, but use it sparingly because an overdose will cause the soil to be excessively alkaline.

Once your hot peppers are finally bearing fruit and if for some foolish reason you're overrun with bravado, keep a small first-aid station handy prior to the first bite. But forget the jug of water. Water doesn't mix with the capsaicin oil, but rather spreads the burning oil around your mouth. Milk and ice cream are far better allies because they both contain a protein called casein, which is quite effective in neutralizing the oil. Bread and rice also work rather well by absorbing capsaicin. It may also help to avoid eating the placenta (the interior white ribs that run down the middle and along the sides of the fruit). Capsaicin is concentrated in the placenta but more or less randomly distributed throughout the rest of the fruit. Since the seeds are in close proximity to the placenta, they tend to pick up a fair bit of oil and can be extremely hot.

It's interesting to note that birds aren't at all sensitive to capsaicin. Apparently, since the digestive system of birds allows the passage of pepper seeds unharmed, peppers and birds have developed something of a symbiotic relationship over time. The mammalian digestive tract, on the other hand, is rather injurious to pepper seeds, and the capsaicin oil probably exists as a simple and effective deterrent to foraging mammals.

So then why have some of the most highly evolved mammals developed such a love affair for scorching hot peppers? That's the burning question.

I WROTE THIS ARTICLE IN THE FINAL DAYS OF A LONG, LINGERING SUMMER, WARM DAYS WITH COOL NIGHTS THAT THREATENED TO FREEZE OUR VEGETABLES INTO USELESS, BITTER PULP. MY SON BILL CHIDED ME A LITTLE WHEN HE READ THIS ARTICLE–IN PARTICULAR THE SECTION ON "GARBAGE IN, GARBAGE OUT". "MOM, YOU'RE TERRIBLE AT THROWING VEGETABLES AWAY," HE SAID, REFERRING TO MY ADVICE TO THROW AWAY ANY VEGETABLES WITH SIGNS OF ROT. I HAVE TO ADMIT THAT HE'S RIGHT: IN THIS PARTICULAR CASE, I FIND IT HARD TO PRACTISE WHAT I PREACH. WHEN IT COMES TO HARVESTING VEGETABLES, DO AS I SAY, NOT AS I DO. OTHERWISE, YOU COULD WIND UP WITH A HAMPER FULL OF ROTTING POTATOES, LIKE I DID!

Vegetable Storage

✴ ORIGINALLY PUBLISHED OCTOBER 18, 1997 ✴

When someone works diligently all summer long to sow a beautiful crop of vegetables, it's understandable that the first blast of cold autumn air can cause a great deal of anxiety. What usually ensues is a bout of panic harvesting, in which gardeners scurry outside and frantically strip all the remaining vegetables from the patch, stuff them into old sacks, boxes and bags, and then unceremoniously toss them in the basement or garage. Inevitably, a large portion of the vegetables rot and eventually end up in the garbage or compost.

The first rule of fall harvesting—and I know it's difficult—is to stay calm. After all, most of the very frost-sensitive vegetables like corn, beans, and tomatoes have already been picked, and nearly all of the remaining vegetables are remarkably frost tolerant. In fact, the flavour of vegetables like rutabagas, brussels sprouts, and parsnips improves substantially after exposure to a few hard frosts. Cold air tends to reduce the slight bitter taste inherent in these three vegetables as well as contributing to an increase in sugar content. While the flavour of other cool-season crops like carrots, cabbage, and broccoli does not improve with freezing weather, neither does it diminish.

Yet there is one compelling reason for leaving these vegetables in the garden for as long as possible into the fall and that is, quite simply, that basements and garages are too warm for most crops. Even cold basements seldom drop below 12 or 14°C, while most vegetables keep best at temperatures just slightly above freezing. Squash, pumpkins, and potatoes are exceptions to the rule. Squash and pumpkins require temperatures around 10 to 12°C, while potatoes store best at 5 to 8°C.

Now, don't get me wrong. I'm not advocating that vegetables should be left in the garden until the final moment before winter freeze-up, but definitely consider leaving them in the patch a little later, particularly if your storage area is less then ideal. Also, keep in mind that although some vegetables—like lettuce, onions, cauli-flower, and broccoli—will tolerate several degrees of frost, extended periods at very cold temperatures in the garden could cause them to break down in storage.

Squash and pumpkins are examples of crops that can tolerate only a very light frost on the mature fruit. Colder temperatures penetrate the skin, causing water-soaked patches that lead to rapid collapse of the fruit. Potato tubers are also sensitive to frost but are insulated from cold by the soil. But be forewarned. Any tubers that may be exposed to the air because of weathering of the hills or cracks in the soil are very prone to freezing and will rot very quickly in storage.

Unfortunately, I learned this lesson the hard way back when my husband Ted and I first began market gardening. An unseasonably early cold snap one autumn froze the odd potato here and there in our potato field. Assuming that the damage was negligible, we harvested the entire crop of near fifty tons and piled them into our root cellar. By January, virtually every single potato had shrunk into a stinking, fetid mass, the smell of which I shall never forget.

This incident indelibly etched rule number two in my mind: "Garbage in, garbage out." Always be particularly vigilant at harvest time and select only blemish-free vegetables for storage. Remember that vegetables never improve in storage. Blemishes that initially appear to be rather insignificant rapidly enlarge from bacterial and fungal breakdown, leading to the collapse of the infected vegetable or, worse, rotting of the entire pile. The best course of action to take with blemished vegetables is to discard the affected part and then use the rest of the vegetable fairly quickly.

Be very careful not to bruise vegetables at any point during harvest. Squash, pumpkins, and potatoes are notoriously prone to storage rot if they've been bumped or dropped during handling. In fact, to prevent bruising injury, no produce should be dropped from a height greater then 15 cm at any time.

Keep in mind that some vegetables store best when they've been heat cured for a few days prior to storage. Heat curing involves simply leaving certain vegetables in a warm, dry room for a day or two prior to storage, to set the skins. For example, squash stores best after it's been cured for several days at 26°C, while onions cured at 35°C for a day, then stored at near freezing, can keep for up to 8 months.

One simple and interesting way to evaluate your storage area is to "read" potato tubers. Potatoes are terrific for providing feedback on how well they have been treated during storage. They are like small biological recorders of their environment. For example, if they are too warm, they will sprout; if they get too cold, they taste sweet; if they turn green, they have been exposed to light; if they turn black in the centre, they can't breathe; if they lose a lot of weight, it's too dry; and so on.

If storing vegetables sounds difficult, don't get discouraged. With any luck, by next spring, you could be pulling your last carrot from the basement on the same day that you dig your first new baby carrot of the season.

ALTHOUGH I WROTE THIS ARTICLE IN THE FALL, SOME OF ITS LESSONS
ON THE IMPORTANCE OF LIGHT APPLY ALL YEAR. AS I WRITE THIS IN
MAY 2000, FOR EXAMPLE, LOW LIGHT LEVELS DUE TO A GREY AND
CLOUDY SPRING HAVE CAUSED SOME OF OUR BEGONIA PLANTS TO SET
THEIR TUBERS PREMATURELY. THE SUN HAS A PROFOUND EFFECT ON
PLANT GROWTH, AND IN THIS ARTICLE I SHARED SOME OF MY INSIGHTS
ON THE SUBJECT, WITH SOME ABLE HELP FROM MY SON JIM.

The Light Fantastic

✴ ORIGINALLY PUBLISHED SEPTEMBER 26, 1998 ✴

Fall is here. For most of us, it isn't the date on the calendar that
heralds the change in seasons; it's the fact that by the time we eat
supper, the sun is slipping below the horizon. The days are shrink-
ing inexorably as autumn creeps back into our lives. The plants can
feel it, too: day length is one of the few environmental factors that
plants can count on to follow a consistent annual pattern. Unlike
moisture, temperature, and wind, the gradual lengthening and
shortening of days follows a regular, rhythmic pattern that many
plants use to prepare for seasonal changes. This phenomenon is
called *photoperiodism.*

Familiarity with photoperiodism is critical for those in the business of growing plants, and it's good information for the home gar-

dener, too. With this year's equinox—one of the major signals plants use to change their growth habits—just behind us, it's a good time to examine how day length influences plant growth. Fortunately, I have my son Jim around to give me a hand with the technical details.

Plants are divided into three categories when we discuss their response to day length: short-day plants, long-day plants, and day-neutral plants. Short-day plants flower only when the daylight period is less than twelve hours. Poinsettias are one such plant. Long-day plants, like spinach, need more than twelve hours of daylight before they flower. Finally, day-neutral plants (like the relatively new day-neutral strawberry varieties) use markers other than day length to determine flowering times.

Here's an example of photoperiodism in action. If you take a look outside right now, chances are you'll see some of the leaves on deciduous trees changing colour. This gorgeous phenomenon is a direct result of photoperiodism. As the days get shorter, the trees absorb the chlorophyll from their leaves. This allows the remaining colour pigments, called carotenoids, to dominate. The absence of the green chlorophyll is what allows other colours to emerge come fall. Warmer fall weather allows for better development of these carotenoids, resulting in more vibrant colours. I'm already enjoying some great displays here on the farm. (I should point out that many academics now note that it's not really the day length, but the hours of darkness that control these changes. It sounds like semantics to me, but I'll take their word for it.)

A little later on this year, the poinsettias growing in our green-house will begin to change colour—once they experience more than twelve hours of darkness per day. The darkness acts as a trigger, initiating flower development; eight to eleven weeks later (depending on the variety), the bracts will have changed from green to red (or pink, or white, or yellow, again, depending on the variety). The 'Freedom' variety of poinsettias is what we call an eight-week crop. That is, flowers are initiated by twelve-hour nights, and eight weeks later the red flowers are completely formed. Since September 21 is the first day with a twelve-hour night, November 16—eight weeks later—is when our poinsettias will be ready. But what if November 16 is too early for blooming? In that case, we can artificially delay blooming by making the days longer with the use of lights. If we light the crop for two weeks, starting September 21, the flowers won't change colour until December 1—just in time for the beginning of the Christmas rush. The process operates like clockwork, but you do have to know what you're doing: if you light the poinsettias for too long, you'll wind up with green poinsettias for Christmas. Understanding photoperiodism can mean the difference between a crop you can sell and one that's practically worthless!

Once spring returns, day length again comes into play. Imagine yourself in a greenhouse next year, picking out perennials for your garden. It isn't always easy. Sure, the plant is right there in front of you, but if you're shopping early in the season, it probably isn't blooming yet because the days haven't gotten long enough to signal the plant to flower. Many greenhouses provide full-colour photographs of their plants in full bloom, but pictures can't compete with taking a close look at the real thing. Imagine being able to see flowers in full bloom before you buy...

It's already happening. Jim recently ran across some research on ways to get perennials to flower earlier than normal. The technique is called "forcing." In the greenhouse, long-day perennials are given additional hours of light at the beginning of the season, forcing them to flower much earlier than their unlit counterparts. Customers browsing through the greenhouse are then able to see the plants in full bloom in the early spring, giving them a better idea of what would look good in their garden. Of course, this also means that the blooming period will be over earlier, since it started earlier; the number of blooming days remains the same. The following year, under natural outdoor conditions, the blooming start and end times will "reset," returning to normal. I think you can expect to see more and more perennials blooming out of season in the future as growers continue to experiment. (Forcing is quite common with bulbs, especially tulips, but hasn't been used for the vast majority of perennials until very recently.)

Plants aren't the only living things that react to day length. Many kinds of insects also take their cues from the onset of darkness. Thrips, for example, are tiny, slender insects that love to eat flowers like gladiolus, but they stop feeding rather abruptly when the days get short enough. This takes a lot of pressure off plants—and off greenhouse workers! I'm always glad to see these pests fade away with the summer. Too bad we can't get them to leave a little earlier...

There is still much that is not understood about photoperiodism; it's one of the most complex phenomena in the gardening field. However, experimentation continues, so it likely won't be long before scientists shed some more light on the subject.

I WROTE THIS ARTICLE A COUPLE OF YEARS AGO, WHEN THERE WAS A SUDDEN SURGE IN THE NUMBER OF POTTING MIXES BECOMING AVAILABLE TO COMMERCIAL GROWERS. ONE OF THE MIXES I WAS PARTICULARLY IMPRESSED WITH WAS COCONUT HUSK FIBRE, MENTIONED NEAR THE END OF THIS STORY. UNFORTUNATELY, THE SUPPLY AND CONSISTENCY OF COCONUT HUSK FIBRE HAS BEEN ERRATIC, WHICH IS TOO BAD; IT HELD GREAT PROMISE. THERE ARE STILL PLENTY OF DIFFERENT MIXES TO CHOOSE FROM, AND I CONTINUE TO EXPERIMENT WITH DIFFERENT POTTING SOILS TO THIS DAY.

Potting Soil Power

༄ ORIGINALLY PUBLISHED NOVEMBER 8, 1997 ༄

I'm stating here and now that potting soil does not receive the respect it so rightfully deserves. Potting soil has no flash—no sparkle or charisma the way a hot new perennial or shrub variety has—but it is quite literally the foundation for healthy plant growth. Everyone who gardens eventually buys a bag or two for repotting house plants or filling patio planters, yet far too often the plants slowly deteriorate simply because their roots are struggling in a soil ill suited for sustaining growth.

And I should know. Over the years I've killed more than my fair share of plants simply because I underestimated the importance of the relationship between plant health and soil quality.

Up until about 30 years ago, most professional growers used a large proportion of field soil in their mixtures. Peat moss and sand were added to lighten and loosen up the often excessively dense field soil. Although these amendments made the mixture lighter, it was still oppressively heavy, and field soils contained weeds, insects, and diseases. Besides, field soil was rather variable—all that was consistent about it was its inconsistency! These problems eventually led to the advent of modern potting soils.

Modern potting soils are somewhat enigmatic. To begin with, they contain absolutely no soil, and, surprising as it may seem, the largest proportion of the mixture, by volume, is air. The best-quality potting blends typically contain nothing more than peat moss, a popped volcanic rock called perlite, perhaps a little bit of a clay-like particle called vermiculite, some horticultural lime, and maybe a bit of fertilizer.

I must admit that because these new soilless mixtures were seemingly so simple, I was more than a little skeptical about their suitability for growing plants. Both my husband and sons were keen to embrace this new technology, but because of my trepidation, we decided not to eliminate field soil from our mixture overnight. So, over a three-year period, we gradually reduced the percentage of field soil from around forty percent to zero with no discernable reduction in plant health.

But although switching from soil-based media to soilless was successful for me, it required some careful scrutiny of the ingredients to grow healthy plants. The problem with soilless mixtures is that they are highly variable and currently no quality standards exist to insure that gardeners are getting a top-notch product. The only way to assess potting soil is to dive into a bag, both hands forward. The best potting soils contain "blond" peat moss, alluding to the fact that it was extracted from the top layers of the peat bog. Blond peat moss is composed of long, fibrous strands that are not only excellent for holding moisture but also contribute to good aeration. Lower in the bog is dark peat, which is partially decomposed and too dense for use in containers.

Perlite, those white, popcorn-like particles, is incorporated into potting soils for drainage and aeration. Since perlite is a relatively expensive component, it may be used far too sparingly in poor-quality mixes. Potting soil should, on average, have about twenty percent perlite blended in, giving the mixture a fairly light feel. The perlite particles should also be rather large, about twice the size of peppercorns. Smaller particles indicate that perhaps they spent too long in the mixer and were crushed excessively. Particles that are too small tend to clog the mixture's pore spaces.

Vermiculite may or may not be included in the mixture. The wafer-like structure of vermiculite provides an ideal trap for moisture and nutrients, and is excellent for inclusion in patio planters. However, vermiculite tends to become a little too soggy for indoor use. Like perlite, vermiculite particle-size is very important. Only long-strand, horticultural-grade vermiculite should be used to prevent the soilless media from becoming too dense.

And don't think that because you place a layer of gravel in the bottom of your pots you've resolved your drainage problem. This common misconception has been around for years. Surprisingly, gravel actually makes the problem worse. Gravel shortens the height of the soil column, and the shorter the height, the worse the drainage.

I mentioned earlier that one of the primary components of soil is air. Always buy mixtures by volume, never by weight. Air is absolutely crucial for root growth, and heavy potting soils cannot be "fluffed" into porous mixtures.

Even though peat, perlite, and vermiculite blends have become the premier potting mixtures, many new and promising products are gaining prominence. One that I've had a fair bit of success with is coconut husk fibre, commonly referred to as coir. It has excellent porosity as well as good water-holding capacity, and it works well in hanging baskets. However, it tends to be a bit heavier than peat-based mixes, and it requires a little more nitrogen fertilizer to produce equivalent plant growth.

Whichever soil you use, just remember that the reason plants are vigorous and healthy can often be found just below the surface.

———— BEST ADVICE————
on successful seeding...
The right sowing dates • Sampling new varieties • Quality seed

EVERY YEAR, SEVERAL OF MY FAMILY MEMBERS MAKE TRIPS DOWN TO
HORTICULTURAL CONFERENCES TO CHECK OUT THE LATEST ADVANCES IN
THE GREENHOUSE BUSINESS. ON ONE SUCH TRIP, MY SON BILL AND
MY DAUGHTER-IN-LAW VALERIE ATTENDED A CONFERENCE IN CHICAGO
THAT HIGHLIGHTED ADVANCES IN SEED TECHNOLOGY. THEIR EXPERIENCES
IN CHICAGO INSPIRED ME TO GIVE MY READERS A CHANCE TO LEARN A
LITTLE ABOUT THE FASCINATING WORLD OF MODERN SEED SCIENCE.

Seed Technology

⁂ ORIGINALLY PUBLISHED JANUARY 17, 1998 ⁂

Maybe I'm a little crazy but, given the choice, I'd much rather
lounge on my chesterfield with a load of seed catalogues on my lap
than bake in the sun on a remote tropical beach. For me, discovering a new plant variety in some obscure European seed catalogue is
far more alluring than feeling warm tradewinds on my face, even in
January.

But while new plant varieties catch my eye, it's the advances in
seed technology that capture my fancy. When my husband Ted and
I first began growing plants for a living, sowing seed was rather
straightforward: choose high-quality seed, place it at the correct
depth in some good soil, provide the appropriate soil temperature
for the prescribed number of days, and hope for the best. Invariably,

some varieties of seed emerged rapidly and vigorously, while others languished. When a particular seed variety consistently failed to produce a significant number of seedlings, we just categorized it as a poor performer. Eventually, with a lot of trial and error and greater knowledge about the requirement on some of the notoriously challenging varieties, we were able to increase our success rate. Today, advances in seed technology are changing the very meaning of the term success.

For us, success was getting half of the seeds to sprout and produce healthy mature plants. And although 50% may have been outstanding for that particular variety, the ultimate goal of everyone who grows from seed is to come as close to the elusive 100% mark as possible. Some major seed companies are making a concerted effort to narrow this gap.

Seed companies evaluate seed field by field. Identical seed varieties may vary in quality because they may have been grown in fields hundreds of miles apart; under different growing conditions, the viability of the seed can vary widely. That's why the fields are often separated, assigned different batch numbers, and tested for germination. The number of sprouted seeds is counted and a germination percentage is assigned to each batch.

Once germination has been evaluated, the germination percentage is stamped on the seed packet or at the very least is kept on file. If the percentage test shows that a batch of seed is not performing up to a high enough standard, the seed may be rejected entirely. The germination test assures the consumer that if the seed contained in a packet is provided with the proper environment, the number stamped on the package is the smallest percentage of seeds that will germinate.

The one problem with germination tests is that testing tells only part of the story. Researchers have taken a close look at germination figures and realized that they are really only a guideline as to how the resulting plants will perform in the real world.

The main problem with germination percentages is that, although they indicate the number of viable seeds in a batch, viability is not necessarily indicative of the number of seeds that will grow to produce healthy plants. Viability simply means that a seed is capable of absorbing moisture and then subsequently starting the process of germination. But it by no means implies that a healthy seedling will emerge and grow up to become a healthy mature plant. Viability is merely a starting point. Seed vigour is what counts.

Viable seed will sprout, but some seedlings may be misshapen or stunted and die a few days after germination. Seed that has vigour, however, will sprout and produce healthy plants.

Up until now, ascertaining which characteristics of a seedling lead to a healthy mature plant has been difficult. However, a company out of Chicago called Ball Seed is determined to change all this. Ball researchers have painstakingly examined thousands of seedlings from germination to maturity, and assessed which seedling characteristics are benchmarks of a healthy mature plant. Researchers analyzed the seedlings for colour, symmetry, and leaf-expansion rate, then fed the results into a computer. Once the computer had these benchmarks, a sample from a batch of seed could be grown to the seedling stage and a scanner used to determine which were likely to have sufficient vigour.

This advancement in seed technology is so extraordinary that Ball Seed had patented the process and called it the Ball Vigour Index™. It's not unusual to find Ball Vigour Indexed seed to have viable and vigorous seed approaching the 99% mark. Unfortunately, because the task of setting the parameters for each seed variety is so onerous, only a handful of varieties fall within the vigour index. As yet none of this seed has worked its way down to the retail shelves, but I'm sure it will soon.

Until it does, the best way to achieve a high rate of success with purchased seed is to pay the extra few cents and get the highest-quality seed. When you consider that the potential success or failure of a plant is wrapped up in a seed that may be no bigger than the head of pin, purchasing high-quality seed is the only option.

I think my mother-in-law had it right. Whenever one of her family or friends asked for advice on buying something, she always said, "Only the rich can afford to buy cheap things." As they say on television, you're worth it—and so is your garden.

A NUMBER OF YEARS AGO, SOME EUROPEAN FRIENDS OF MINE SCOFFED
AT THE BIG POTATOES I RAISED. "THAT IS WHAT YOU USE TO FEED THE PIGS!"
THEY SAID, AND EXPLAINED HOW MUCH TASTIER TINY POTATOES ARE.
WELL, I LIKE POTATOES LARGE AND SMALL, BUT RECALLING THIS
STORY INSPIRED ME TO EXPLORE THE NOTION THAT, IN THE
GARDENING WORLD, BIGGER ISN'T ALWAYS BETTER.

Thinking Small

⁂ ORIGINALLY PUBLISHED APRIL 11, 1998 ⁂

We all know the rule, right? Bigger is better. Well, with plants, it ain't necessarily so. How many of us have discovered that our prized old tree has grown so high that it threatens our power lines or throws shade over the entire yard? And what about fruit trees? They can grow so huge that picking fruit from the upper branches starts to resemble a trip to the top of Mount Everest. When fewer and fewer of us can afford large yards, or even to buy a house at all, apartment dwellers and others who don't want to give up—or who have never even had the chance to try—their favourite plant varieties are looking for new ways to approach these difficulties. Take heart: for every problem, there is a solution. A number of familiar favourites are becoming available in dwarf varieties.

On the prairies, for example, you'll find the new dwarf apple trees. The trees come in the regular varieties that you'd normally expect—Harcourt, Battleford, Norland, and others—but these familiar scions are grafted onto a special hardy dwarf rootstock called Ottawa. The trees grow to about 70% of the height of a typical apple tree, but they bear a heavy crop, usually fruiting within two years of planting. Fruit also develops earlier in the season than the standard varieties. The apples are as large, great-tasting, and juicy as those grown on the regular-size trees; only the tree itself is small in stature. This reduced size also makes it hardier since excessively lush growth often contributes to greater winter damage. Picking fruit is so easy that it's almost sinful. No ladders are necessary - just reach out and grab an apple. Dwarf apple trees, though, are a little shorter-lived than their larger cousins, usually lasting about twenty-five years before going gently into that good night. As a final note, don't forget that, like all apple trees, each dwarf variety must be cross-pollinated (it doesn't have to be by another dwarf!) in order to bear fruit. Either plant two different varieties in your yard or make sure that a nearby neighbour has one.

Another way to grow dwarf trees is to pursue the thousand-year-old Japanese art of bonsai, which really began to catch on here in the West in the early 1980s. Its popularity has been rising steadily over the years, despite - or perhaps because of - the challenge of growing an eye-catching miniature tree. Bonsai simply means "a plant in a tray"; the small size of the tree is maintained by the confinement of the pot, by pinching off top growth, and by pruning the roots. The desired result is to reach a balance between the foliage and the roots, while at the same time developing a satisfactory shape in one of the popular styles: formal upright, twin trunk, weeping, windswept, slanting, cascade, and so on.

The traditional bonsai tree is a hardy variety (pines, maples, junipers, etc.) which is planted and kept outdoors; a recent Western innovation is the indoor bonsai. Indoor bonsai include tender varieties like weeping figs, parasol plants, and umbrella trees. Don't try to grow an indoor variety outdoors or vice-versa, but do remember that both types need to be occasionally exposed to both environments. That is, take your indoor bonsai outside once in a while during the summer, and pull your outdoor plants indoors during cold snaps. Bonsai trees require a lot of care, including daily waterings and frequent pruning, but the payoff is substantial: a healthy bonsai plant tends to impress. Nurturing bonsai almost makes you part gardener, part sculptor, and part frantic parent. It's a wonderful combination of contrasting art forms and skills.

Sunflowers have been mainstays on farm fences for decades. They have a serene, stately beauty, due mainly to their impressive size. However, not even the traditional perception of this grand old flower is immune to change. New, smaller sunflowers are peeking over the horizon. For example, there's the well-named Big Smile variety, a beautiful, golden-yellow flower with a deep-black centre. Big Smiles are typically about 30 to 38 cm tall, with 15-cm wide heads. I especially recommend these for children's gardens; they also make great border plants. The Teddy Bear is another small sunflower I enjoy. At 90 cm (3 ft.) tall, this one's a bit taller than the Big Smile, but still only half the size of the gargantuan Russian Mammoth. Teddy Bears are fast-growing, bushy, and quite sturdy, with fully double, bright-yellow flowers that are about the same size as the Big Smile's. This is another good border plant. The Teddy Bear variety is similar to the one shown in Van Gogh's famous painting. Another great quality of dwarf sunflowers is that they will thrive quite nicely in containers; you don't have to have a garden to enjoy them. Just make sure that they're not shaded: sunflowers, as the name suggests, need a good dose of direct sunlight every day, so choose your location accordingly.

In recent years, gardeners have made great strides with small plants. Thinking big is all well and good, but sometimes thinking small pays off even bigger.

ONE OF THE MOST COMMON QUESTIONS IN THE FALL IS,
"WHAT'S THE BEST WAY TO OVERWINTER MY GERANIUMS?"
SOMETIMES THESE ARTICLES NEED TO COVER THE BASICS,
SO I DECIDED TO RECORD MY BEST HINTS ON THE SUBJECT.

Zonal Geraniums
All Year Round

✣ ORIGINALLY PUBLISHED FEBRUARY 22, 1997 ✣

Zonal or cutting geraniums (*Pelargonium hortorum*) are not only
one of the most popular bedding plants in North America but,
inadvertently, also one of the most common houseplants.

Mind you, the title of most common houseplant is due entirely
to the fact that we're so reluctant to part with them once the frosts
come in fall, and thousands of them end up stored in basements for
the winter. By February they aren't much to look at, but provided
they receive a little light and are kept cool during winter, they do
store quite well and can be rejuvenated quite rapidly. Rejuvenation
should begin now so that the zonal geraniums will be well established prior to planting in May.

Ninety percent of the 250 or so species of geraniums are indigenous to warm, sunny, fairly dry regions of southern Africa. Not surprisingly, the two most critical factors for re-growth of the plants are bright light and warm temperature—essentially the reverse of winter storage conditions. Unless you have a small greenhouse or solarium that is naturally well lit, geraniums should be placed as close to a south-facing window as possible. Keep in mind that even in a south-facing window, plants receive a meager 1/100th of the amount of sunlight they would receive outdoors on a bright day, and since light is the driving force behind plant growth, every additional bit of light they receive is important. Grow lights will help regardless of where the geraniums are located.

Once you've found a nice, bright location, the geranium's roots should be cleaned of all garden soil and re-potted into a loose, peat moss-based soilless mixture to encourage rapid root and shoot growth. Beyond the fact that the geraniums will grow much more vigorously in a light, peaty mixture, garden soil often contains disease and insect pests.

After the geraniums have been transplanted, fertilizing can begin. I like to use a half-strength solution of 10-52-10 (10 ml in 5 litres) once a week until the new shoots are about 6 or 7 cm long. Once the shoots reach this length, it's decision time. At this point, either the geranium plants can be nurtured along until May and then simply transplanted outside, or the now vigorous "mother" plant can be harvested of its cuttings. The best approach is to harvest the cuttings. Mother plants are often tough and woody and lack the symmetry and vigour of cuttings. Reasonably energetic mother plants grown in the home will yield about half a dozen cuttings each. In some commercial greenhouses, huge tree-like mother plants are grown year-round and can yield up to 300 cuttings annually.

Cuttings can either be removed with a knife or simply snapped off. Either way, once the cuttings are removed, they should be left on a counter top to dry for a couple of hours. Drying enables the cut end to develop a strong, disease-resistant layer of cells called suberin. Without that suberized layer, it is not uncommon to lose all of the cuttings to stem-rot diseases.

The cuttings can now be stuck back into a peat-soil mixture, but a far better approach is to push the unrooted cuttings into sterile foam blocks called "oasis" cubes. These cubes are free of diseases and provide the optimum balance of moisture and air for strong root development. (One additional note on rooting: avoid attempting to root geranium cuttings in water. Oxygen is as critical to rooting as moisture is, but water contains very little dissolved oxygen and rooting can be exceedingly slow, if it happens at all. As well, the water can literally become a bacterial cesspool after only a few days.)

The "stuck" cuttings should be returned to a brightly lit spot and placed on a heat register or heating cable, to warm the root zone to about 22 to 24°C. It's easy to see if the geranium cuttings are on the right track: the cut end should swell and form a callus after a few days. Once a callus forms, the roots will emerge shortly thereafter.

After the cuttings produce roots 5 to 7 cm long, they should be transplanted into pots 10 to 12 cm in diameter, containing a pasteurized, peat moss-based mixture. Fertilizing can now be resumed, preferably with a complete fertilizer like 10-52-10, again at half strength.

By mid April, the geraniums can be taken outside during the day as long as temperatures are 15°C or warmer. Don't put the geraniums in full sunlight outdoors because the leaves are not acclimatized to direct sunlight and can easily burn. A bright, indirect sunlit area on a deck is best.

With any luck, most, if not all, of the cuttings should be vigorous, multi-branched plants ready for transplanting outside in May. At the very least, they'll be a lot better looking than they were during winter.

on some of my favourite introductions...
Tumbler tomatoes • *Wave petunias* • *Dragon Wing begonias*

EVERY YEAR, MY DAUGHTER-IN-LAW VALERIE RIGOROUSLY TESTS HUNDREDS OF NEW PLANT VARIETIES, EVALUATING THEM ON THEIR BEAUTY, DISEASE RESISTANCE, GARDEN PERFORMANCE, AND A NUMBER OF OTHER QUALITIES. WATCHING HER PERFORM THOSE TRIALS HAS HELPED ME LEARN HOW HARD PLANT BREEDERS HAVE TO WORK TO COME UP WITH TRULY NEW AND SPECTACULAR PLANT VARIETIES. THIS ARTICLE IS DEDICATED TO THE HARDWORKING GROWERS BEHIND THE SCENES—THE UNSUNG HEROES OF TODAY'S GARDENS.

New Varieties Don't Grow On Trees

✤ ORIGINALLY PUBLISHED NOVEMBER 7, 1997 ✤

At this time of year, with the garden put away, I'm usually wandering through the poinsettias, marvelling at the vibrant colours emerging from the foliage. Or I'll be nestled safely inside Edmonton's Winspear Centre, enjoying the symphony. And I'll spend many hours leafing through the catalogues of the various seed companies, admiring the dozens of new plants that will be available next spring, hoping they'll turn out to be good performers.

An abundance of varieties is something I've come to take for granted. However, bringing new varieties to market is the culmination of years, or even decades, of effort. Breeders are continuously chasing after what could be called the "Holy Grails" of gardening: the blue rose, the black tulip, yellow impatiens. (Heck, I can't wait to see them myself!) Sometimes their determination results in fantastic new varieties that take the world by storm, but just as often the experiments are fruitless. In plant breeding, there's a razor-thin line between success and failure. And when I reflect on the many plants I've seen travel that line, the first example that comes to mind is impatiens—probably because I can see them outside my window even now. Some of these lovely pink beauties are blooming in protected areas near the house, though the snow I see filtering down from above will probably finish them off.

A few months ago, our greenhouse was filled with hundreds of the New Guinea variety of impatiens. Most gardeners are familiar with these large-flowered, mounding plants; they come in a wide variety of colours and perform very well in flowerbeds and hanging baskets. New Guinea impatiens have been available in Canada for over twenty years, but it's only been in the last five years or so that its popularity has exploded. The reason? The New Guinea impatiens of old wasn't spectacular, yet a few visionary breeders recognized its tremendous untapped potential. Through relentless cross-breeding, they created the plant with the large and plentiful flowers we admire today.

It was nineteenth-century explorers who first stumbled across the yet-to-be-named impatiens species on the South Pacific island of New Guinea. They were very impressed by their large flowers and big, showy leaves. The real beginning of the New Guinea impatiens' rise to gardening stardom, however, wasn't until an American expedition returned to the island in 1970. From the specimens gathered on that trip, today's impatiens would spring—but only after many hurdles were jumped. The challenge was to force the New Guinea impatiens to conform to our standards of beauty. The breeders wanted to develop a plant that had lots of flowers and a more compact form to make it suitable for beds and hanging baskets. Concerns over disease resistance and vigour also had to be addressed. Even assigning it a proper name was contentious. (We seem to have settled on *Impatiens* x 'New Guinea' as a Latin name, although some scientists feel that something more accurate is needed.)

Thousands of crosses of different types of New Guineas were necessary to develop the plants of today. When promising strains were established, over 100 universities and dozens of commercial growers throughout North America were given cuttings. From these cuttings, the growers developed over 200 impatiens varieties in a wide range of colours and growth habits. The proper cultural requirements for impatiens took some time. Trials were run, with plants being given different amounts of light, water, and fertilizer; from these trials, growers were able to determine which combinations produced the best-quality plants.

Even after all of that tedious work, though, breeders face the most terrifying prospect of all: what if the retailers don't like the plant? We participated in several New Guinea impatiens trials back in the early 1980s, assessing the plants for vigour, colour, and garden performance. When the New Guineas finally came into full flower, I was a little disappointed and my son Bill hated them with a passion. ("Looks like a ratty old bush," I remember him saying.) It took several more years of intensive breeding before we received a variety that we felt was attractive enough to sell. Judging by the hundreds of thousands of New Guinea impatiens sold today, I'd say that the new varieties can be legitimately deemed a success.

Not all endings are quite this happy, though. I remember when the first double-flowering impatiens series, the highly touted 'Rosebud' impatiens, burst onto the scene. The Rosebud breeders experienced many of the same difficulties that the New Guinea impatiens breeders faced, but ultimately the problems with this new double-flowered variety were too numerous. Although the Rosebud series was showcased by hopeful breeders, it soon became apparent to professional growers and home gardeners alike that Rosebuds were destined to fail. These impatiens had a tendency to get woody and thick, they were prone to viral attack, the colours were dull, not vibrant, and half of the leaves routinely turned yellow and fell off. Perhaps most devastating was the inconsistent flowering: many of the blooms were only single-flowered.

However, the failure of the Rosebud impatiens provided important lessons for breeders. It became an important step in the development of the double-flowered impatiens variety that did succeed: the 'Fiesta' impatiens, now a popular Mother's Day gift. Sometimes, failure breeds success.

Despite the occasional setback, new varieties continue to be introduced at an astonishing rate. And there's no end in sight: seed catalogues are getting thicker and thicker as the years go by. Our gardens are more vigorous, more colourful, and easier to maintain than ever before. I think it's fair to say that the hard work of plant breeders everywhere has helped to make this the Golden Age of gardening.

WHEN I WROTE THIS ARTICLE, HERBAL REMEDIES WERE ALL OVER THE NEWS.
I THOUGHT I SHOULD SHARE MY PERSPECTIVE, AND AS IT TURNED OUT, THIS
PIECE RECEIVED MORE RESPONSES FROM READERS THAN ALMOST ANY OTHER.
WHEN I PUBLISHED MY BOOK ON CULINARY HERBS IN EARLY 2000, I MADE
A CONSCIOUS DECISION NOT TO DISCUSS THE MEDICINAL USES OF HERBS—
PARTLY BECAUSE OF WHAT I LEARNED WHILE WRITING THIS ARTICLE. TOO MANY
OF US SUCCUMB TO THE NOTION THAT WHAT'S NATURAL IS AUTOMATICALLY
SAFE. I WROTE THIS ARTICLE TO ENCOURAGE PEOPLE TO RESPECT THE TREMEN-
DOUS—AND STILL LARGELY UNKNOWN—POWER OF HERBAL MEDICINES

A Cautionary Tale
of Herbal Medicines

ᴥ ORIGINALLY PUBLISHED DECEMBER 19, 1998 ᴥ.

Herbal remedies are all the rage these days, promising to allevi-
ate a wide variety of ills. Many of my friends stock up on ginseng,
gingko, and other herbs, hoping to enhance their health. I always
feel rejuvenated after a hot cup of tea, so I understand the impulse.

One plant in particular, *Echinacea* (also known as purple
coneflower), has taken centre stage in the "cure all that ails you"
category of herbal remedies. However, an emerging problem with

Echinacea and many other herbs is determining the purity and potency of the various herbal products.

At the Alberta Horticultural Congress recently held in Edmonton, a researcher from the University of British Columbia described the problem. She noted that there are many species of *Echinacea*—at least nine in North America. The variety commonly grown in gardens right across Canada is *Echinacea purpurea*. It's one of my favourite flowering plants, but when it comes to fighting disease, this species of *Echinacea* is a lightweight. (However, plant breeders are developing improved varieties of *E. purpurea* that may contain higher levels of the medicinally beneficial compounds.)

Only the species *Echinacea angustifolia* contains large quantities of the chemicals thought of as being essential to the plant's immuno-stimulant qualities: chicoric acid, cynarin, alkylamides, and echinacosides. The other eight or so species are relatively ineffective as medicinal plants. Surprisingly, some commercial growers are still unaware they are growing species of *Echinacea* other than *E. angustifolia*. On some farms, *Echinacea simulata, E. purpurea,* or one of the other species was being grown and innocently but erroneously sold as *E. angustifolia*. Since *E. purpurea* is more than double the size of *E. angustifolia* and produces two to three times the dry matter yield, *E. purpurea* is often the primary species blended into *Echinacea* formulations. I ran over to the drugstore to have a look at a few bottles of *Echinacea* pills; sure enough, most had *E. purpurea* listed as the main species, followed by *E. angustifolia*. However, it's impossible to tell what proportion *E. angustifolia* represents in the bottle from the ingredients—which means that it's also impossible to gauge the medicine's potency.

To cloud the issue even more, a herb's potency is not strictly related to its being the correct species. The correct part of the plant must be harvested and processed. In the case of *Echinacea*, the root is the only part of the plant that contains the medicinally useful compounds in any appreciable quantities. Plants must also be harvested at the proper point in their life cycle. When harvesting gingko, the popular memory-enhancer, for example, growers must wait until the leaves have turned yellow—otherwise, the active ingredients aren't present. (I'm sure commercial growers know this, but some home gardeners giving medicinal herbs a try in their plots may not.) Plus, potency can fade if the herbs are allowed to sit in storage for too long or if they are improperly packaged.

One of the biggest problems is the variability among plants within a species. Since plants are complex organisms, it's difficult to get repeatable experimental results from one individual plant to another. An identical test on two individuals of the same species might produce the expected identical results—or it might not. To fight this problem, scientists select a chemical "marker" that is characteristic of a particular plant species and, they hope, indicative of the plant's potency. Unfortunately, chemical markers are sometimes discovered to have a much weaker link to the medicinal properties of the plant than originally supposed. This issue must be addressed to ensure that we are getting what we pay for when we purchase herbal products.

Purity of a herbal medicine can have a dramatic impact on the potency of the product. For example, fillers are often added—usually starches, chalk, or other harmless additives. These additives serve various purposes, such as providing structure for the pill (making it possible to hold on to) or making the pill large enough to be visible (if the required dosage per pill is very small).

Sometimes, however, additives are included for less benign reasons—that is, to lower the cost to the manufacturer of producing the remedy. This process is called adulteration. Naturally, adulteration also reduces the potency of the remedy: more dosages are required to have the same effect as a more concentrated, less adulterated herbal. Thus, the manufacturer's profits rise while value to the consumer falls.

Despite these problems, I still feel that herbal medicines may have some potential benefit. A dear friend of mine relied heavily upon traditional remedies. Virginia Durocher, a Metis neighbour, worked on our farm for many years. During that time I saw her use plants to create all kinds of herbal treatments, for everything from colds to headaches. She lived to be ninety-two. Of course, much of her longevity can be attributed to genetics and other factors, but I can't help thinking that her adherence to traditional medicine must have had at least some impact on her robust health. Her example has certainly influenced my own thinking, and in this confusing, contradictory era, it's good to have her memory to call upon.

I WROTE THIS STORY BECAUSE ONE OF MY FAVOURITE CARROT
VARIETIES, FAVOR, HAD JUST BEEN DISCONTINUED. IT UPSET
ME THAT SUCH A TASTY, TENDER CARROT WAS BEING PULLED OFF THE
SHELF SIMPLY BECAUSE IT WAS DIFFICULT TO SHIP WITHOUT BREAKING.
I STILL HAVE A LITTLE SEED LEFT, BUT EVENTUALLY THAT WILL BE GONE,
AND I'LL ONLY HAVE MEMORIES OF A GREAT VEGETABLE.

Falling Out of Favor

ORIGINALLY PUBLISHED FEBRUARY 20, 1999

They've done it again. Every year, it seems that we get at least one notice from the seed companies, announcing which seed lines have been discontinued. The casualty list for 1999 has arrived, and one of my favourite vegetable varieties is on it: the Favor (no "u") carrot. I wouldn't be so upset if this were an old variety being usurped by a new, superior one. Unfortunately, Favor is one of the most stellar performers I've grown in the last few years, and as far as I can see it's not being replaced by anything better. Perhaps the loss of one of my favourite corn varieties a few years back should have warned me that Favor would eventually wind up on the chopping block, too.

Maple Sweet corn, indisputably one of the best hybrid introductions of the last few years, went the way of the dodo about three years ago. With superb flavour and the sweetest, most succulent kernels I've ever tasted, Maple Sweet should have become the gold standard in the garden. It didn't happen.

I'm not sure why Maple Sweet corn was discontinued. I imagine that it was not as popular with commercial growers as some other varieties, perhaps because the cobs are slightly smaller, or because the kernels are fairly delicate and farmers had difficulty with bruised cobs during handling. Whatever the case, it certainly deserved more respect. I'm just thankful that I got some advance warning of the cancellation so that I could stockpile enough seed to last a few years.

I can tell you, however, something about why Favor fell out of favour. The Favor carrot is a beauty, a real gourmet treat. It's sweet and juicy from the baby stage right through to maturity, and was easily the best performer in my vegetable patch last year. Everyone who tried one of these tender delicacies was absolutely wowed by the taste. Now, I almost feel bad for introducing gardeners to this carrot; it seems cruel to offer such a tantalizingly delicious treat only to snatch it away after such a brief interlude.

Back in the 1980s, we operated a wholesale carrot farm. When we started out, Imperator carrots were the industry standard, and they remain so today. They have some great attributes: they're long, straight, and heavy yielding. Unfortunately, they also have the texture of cordwood, and yet Imperators are what you'll find in most grocery stores. The only reason they're so dominant is because they're easy to harvest and ship. Huge mechanical harvesters dig them up and dump them into wagons; Imperator-type carrots are so tough and fibrous that they can take the abuse without breaking.

Frankly, my family has never liked Imperator carrots very much, so instead we decided to grow the much more succulent Nantes 616. Nantes-style carrots (like the later Favor) aren't nearly as tough as Imperators. At the Alberta Crop Diversification Centre in Brooks, they have a "flat plate breakage test" that all trial carrot varieties have to endure. No fancy equipment required for this experiment: just lift a carrot to a height of six feet, drop it onto a flat steel plate, and see if it breaks. Imperators broke very rarely; Nantes shattered 100% of the time.

That's probably what doomed the Favor carrot. Culling broken carrots is very labour intensive and, subsequently, very expensive for the grower. That means Favor carrots, though superior in both flavour and texture, are less profitable than the woody Imperators or those dreadful, enormous, tough Chantenay carrots you find sliced up at cheap buffets. For this reason, the availability of Nantes-type carrots is sporadic. Fortunately, most produce vendors at farmers' markets have a consistent supply from early summer through fall.

I don't mean to be unduly critical, but sometimes I wonder why seed companies bother to release these superior varieties at all. They've become more fickle than the fashion industry. It's no great insight that companies must make money to survive and that nearly every industry has been affected by global competition—but can we slow the pace just a little? I mean, really, one year for Favor carrots?

Having said that, I must be fair (though my family refers to it as "fence riding") to the seed companies. Unexpected problems can arise with promising new seed varieties. I remember a potato cultivar that was released a few years ago—Connestoga. We were very excited about it because it was the earliest-maturing potato ever developed. The plants produced beautiful, round, creamy, white-fleshed tubers that were outstanding baked or as French fries. But to the surprise of everyone—farmers, seed companies, and especially Health Canada—during a cool growing season the Connestoga tubers developed a very bitter taste. When the tubers were analyzed in the lab, they contained exceedingly high levels of poisonous alkaloids called solanin. All potatoes produce solanin naturally, but at levels that aren't typically high enough to poison people. But if a growing season was particularly cold, Connestoga potatoes would produce double the normal amount of alkaloids. Naturally, the seed companies withdrew the variety. It was, of course, the right thing to do, and it must have been financially painful for them.

Perhaps the answer, then, is that we, as consumers, must let the seed companies know when we're impressed with quality seed. Everybody loves a little pat on the back, and who knows? That bit of feedback might be just what it takes for the powers-that-be to keep that great new variety on the market a year or two longer.

THE FIRST HYBRID SEED WE PURCHASED WAS A TOMATO CALLED SUPER
FANTASTIC. IT WAS FAR SUPERIOR TO THE MOST POPULAR VARIETIES OF
THE TIME, MANITOBA AND EARLY CHATHAM, BUT GARDENERS CAN BE
SKEPTICAL WHEN IT COMES TO NEW BREEDS. ONE FELLOW CAME IN
LOOKING FOR EARLY CHATHAM, AND BILL SUGGESTED HE TRY THE NEW
SUPER FANTASTIC INSTEAD. "I'M NOT GONNA BUY THAT," THE CUSTOMER
SAID GRUFFLY, BUT BILL WAS DETERMINED AND GAVE HIM TWO YOUNG
PLANTS GROWN FROM THE HYBRID SEED. HE WAS SO SHOCKED THAT HE
PUT THE EARLY CHATHAM BACK ON THE SHELF AND BOUGHT TWO MORE
SUPER FANTASTIC. PEOPLE STILL SEEM TO NEED A LITTLE CONVINCING
WHEN IT COMES TO THE QUALITIES OF HYBRID SEED, SO I WROTE
THIS ARTICLE IN THE HOPES OF TURNING THEM AROUND.

Hybrid Seeds

✤ ORIGINALLY PUBLISHED FEBRUARY 28, 1998 ✤

Once the prefix "hybrid" is slapped on a package of vegetable
seed, it immediately acquires an air of distinction. But is this lofty
status warranted, or are hybrid varieties just a bunch of seeds that
are over-hyped and over-priced?

My first encounter with hybrid seed dates back far too many
years to mention. I had always grown the non-hybrid corn variety
'Amazing Early Alberta' because, as I was told, "that's what every-

body grows." But my husband Ted and I decided to experiment with a row or two of a new hybrid variety called 'Buttervee.'

Buttervee was touted as having superior flavour, uniformity, and yield, but we reserved a healthy amount of skepticism. As it turned out, Buttervee was a vast improvement over Amazing Early Alberta. It was much sweeter and retained its flavour much longer. I swear that the duration of Amazing Early Alberta's sweetness was best measured with an hourglass.

Since my corn-patch epiphany, many new corn varieties have replaced and indeed surpassed Buttervee, and few species of vegetables remain untouched by hybridization. Today, the vast majority of my garden is devoted to hybrid varieties because of their superior performance.

So what exactly are hybrids? Essentially, hybrids are intensively cultivated and highly uniform varieties of a particular type of plant. Corn is perhaps the most hybridized of all vegetables and the simplest example of how a hybrid variety is developed.

In a rather simplified version of corn hybridization, plant breeders begin with, say, a corn variety that has wonderful sweetness but very short cobs. Another corn variety may have beautiful long cobs but the kernels might taste rather starchy. The trick is to combine the superior traits of both varieties and produce a new variety that has the desirable traits of each—long cobs that taste sweet.

It would seem that the easiest method to achieve this goal would be to allow cross-pollination of the two varieties—let the pollen of the sweet variety fall on the long cobs of the other variety and vice versa. The problem with this technique, referred to more commonly as "open pollination," is that the resulting seed is highly variable. Some seeds may produce long, sweet cobs, but many will not. It's much like human families where the children share common parents but are still quite variable in stature.

Hybridization circumvents this variability problem. Hybrid variety development starts with inbreeding the parents. First, the short cob parent is inbred (only short-cob pollen is allowed to pollinate short cobs) for perhaps 5 to 6 generations. The same inbreeding occurs with the long-cob parent. The result is two highly inbred, highly uniform varieties that are ready to be cross-pollinated. Once the parents are cross-pollinated, if everything goes right, a 100% long, sweet cob variety will result. In addition, the new hybrid variety often exhibits a condition called hybrid vigour, meaning that it is considerably more robust than either of its parents.

Many other vegetables besides corn have undergone hybridization with equally remarkable results. And the same basic principle applies: inbreed the parents, weed out the bad characteristics, keep the good, and then breed the two. There are also many failures on the road to development of a superior hybrid, and hybrid variety development can be much more complex than the corn example.

In Canada, because of our rather short growing season, we can often produce only one generation of any vegetable variety per season. Therefore, seed development often occurs in tropical countries, where several generations can be reared per year. Greenhouses are used to a certain extent on select varieties to further speed seed development. Because hybrid seed production is a rather expensive undertaking, it's not unusual for some hybrid varieties to cost more than double that of their non-hybrid counterparts.

Tomato seed is a prime example. One new hybrid tomato called 'Tumbler' costs an astounding $0.45 per seed. As a result, Tumbler tomato seed is very difficult to find, simply because most people refuse to pay this seemingly exorbitant price.

This is a rather unfortunate situation because, although the seed is expensive, the outstanding yield and flavour of the fruit easily make up for the high seed cost. In a direct competition between Tumbler and a cheaper variety, the value of just one extra Tumbler tomato more than makes up for its more expensive seed.

As I expound the virtues of hybrid seed, one might be led to believe that open-pollinated seed is anachronistic and passé. Nothing could be further from the truth. Old seed varieties possess an extremely valuable pool of genes that have been moulded and shaped by countless years of evolution. Every hybrid variety owes its existence to this gene pool. Some plant varieties that initially appear to have little value for human use may contain highly valuable genes capable of withstanding an assault from some new insidious disease or bug.

So, although I don't expect to save the world from the next corn scourge, I think I'll just keep a small jar of Amazing Early Alberta tucked safely away in my basement.

—— BEST ADVICE ——
my favourite weeding tools...
Stirrup hoe • Walk-behind rototiller • Push hoe

MY SON JIM LOVES HIS TOYS, FROM THE TURBO BOOST IN HIS CAR TO THE
RAYGUN HE CARRIES AROUND TO MEASURE AIR TEMPERATURE IN THE GREEN-
HOUSE. PERSONALLY, I'M A LOW-TECH WOMAN—GIVE ME A RADIO
OVER A COMPUTER ANY DAY. BUT JIM'S ENTHUSIASM HAS RUBBED
OFF A LITTLE, AND I DECIDED TO SHARE MY THOUGHTS ON WHAT I FELT
WERE SOME OF THE ERA'S MOST INTRIGUING GARDENING GIZMOS.

High-Tech Gardening

Ↄ ORIGINALLY PUBLISHED OCTOBER 17, 1998 Ↄ

I admit it: I'm not exactly a whiz when it comes to programming
the VCR, and I'm still not sure how e-mail works. I don't own a cel-
lular phone, and I let my daughter-in-law Valerie set up and maintain
my voice mail. I wouldn't call myself old-fashioned, but I like to pick
and choose which high-tech instruments I allow into my life.

The gardener's tools have always been the hoe, the fork, a keen eye,
and experience. But, as my sons are quick to point out, to stay competitive you've got to keep in touch with the latest developments in
technology. "Mom, we've got equipment in here you don't know
anything about!" they bemoan. So, feeling a bit guilty, I let them bring
me up to speed. My son Jim is very good at keeping me informed,
and here are a few of the latest scientific wonders he has come across.

Plant stress detection glasses are a really neat device based on technology developed by the rocket scientists at NASA. Just slip them on like any old pair of glasses, take a look at your plants, and you'll be able to spot diseases like fire blight on apple trees or conditions like stressed turf before our naked eyes can detect the symptoms. The glasses work by blocking out the green colour reflected by chlorophyll, so healthy areas of the foliage appear black or grey. Where chlorophyll has been reduced by stress, disease, or pests, the plants appear yellowish brown or pink. It's a simple, clever idea that gives growers a chance to correct problems before they become irreversible. They even come as clip-ons! This is the kind of high-tech solution I like—it's simple and relatively cheap. (One pair costs about $75.) No buttons to fiddle with, no controls to calibrate; just put on the glasses and you're ready for action. Apparently, they're also good for pinpointing hot spots during forest fires— something firefighters may appreciate.

An Israeli company, Shany Ray, has developed a more sophisticated tool: the Phytomonitoring System. The device measures changing fruit diameter, stem diameter, carbon dioxide exchange, air temperature, soil temperature and moisture, light levels, and so on. Sensors are clipped to the various plant parts or inserted into the soil, until the plant looks kind of like it's hooked up to a life-support system. The readings are fed into a central computer. If the measurements fall outside the range of what should be normal for the plant, then the computer adjusts the greenhouse environment to match the plant's needs. The Phytomonitoring System is designed for professional growers; a few representative plants are monitored, and any changes in feeding and watering are applied to all of the plants of that type. Stresses are detected early, so adjustments can be made before the plants suffer serious damage. I doubt this kind of system will ever replace hands-on inspection of the plants, but it's nice to have an all-seeing eye keeping watch over them. I like to think of devices like these as back-ups; since you can't be watching your tomatoes 24 hours a day, it's good to know that they're not being left completely unattended.

My son Jim often carries around a raygun, or at least something that looks like one. It's really a point-and-shoot portable thermometer. If an area of the greenhouse feels a little too warm or a little too cold, Jim takes out the raygun and pulls the trigger. He tells me that the gun detects the invisible infrared light which all objects reflect or emit. The gun measures the energy coming from whichever object it's pointed at and then translates that measurement into a temperature reading. Amazing! Jim doesn't rely solely on the device, but it gives him a "second opinion." He also has a portable light meter to measure—naturally—light levels near our plants. These new light meters are really remarkable, because they don't simply measure light; they measure the colours of light that plants actually utilize for growth. While fooling around with the light meter, we noticed something very strange: commercial grow lights, according to the meter, put out no more energy than the common fluorescent lights in our office. Are grow lights any better than plain old house lighting? It's certainly an interesting question...

Once upon a time, growers who suspected their plants were infected with disease had to send plant samples to far-off laboratories for testing; results often took days or weeks to arrive. It wasn't uncommon for a large portion of the crop to perish before confirmation of the problem arrived from the lab. Today, there are a number of kits that allow growers to test right in the field and obtain results in as little as twenty minutes. There are several neatly packaged on-site testing kits available. They cover a wide range of plant diseases, with pretty strange names like Tomato Spotted Wilt Virus, Impatiens Necrotic Spot Virus, Cucumber Mosaic Virus, plus a host of other diseases that affect a wide range of crops. We've tried out some of these kits, and they are very accurate; they're also really easy to use.

I'll probably never use any of these technological wonders myself, but they sure are neat—and they're helping to improve the overall health of the industry, which benefits me even if I never lay hands on the latest gardening gizmo.

Best Advice
on the best light sources in foot candles...
Outdoors–10,000 fc • Greenhouse–1000 fc • South-facing window–500 fc

PLANTS ARE FANTASTIC LIGHT-CONVERTING MACHINES. SO SILENTLY,
SO STEADILY DO PLANTS PERFORM THEIR WORK THAT WE OFTEN FORGET
THAT THE CHANGE OF LIGHT WITH THE SEASONS CAN DISRUPT THEIR
PERFECT FUNCTIONING. THIS ARTICLE WAS INSPIRED BY SOME DISPIRITED-
LOOKING HOUSEPLANTS, PATIENTLY AWAITING THE RETURN OF THE
SUN THROUGH OUR BRIGHT AND FESTIVE HOLIDAY SEASON. TODAY PEOPLE
STILL ASK ABOUT PROPER ILLUMINATION LEVELS FOR INDOOR PLANTS; I HOPE
THE FOLLOWING WILL SHED SOME LIGHT ON THE SUBJECT.

Let There Be Lights

ORIGINALLY PUBLISHED DECEMBER 20, 1997

The spectacular displays of Christmas lights tend to make me forget that we are rapidly approaching the shortest day of the year—the winter solstice.

Outdoor plants are oblivious to the dark season, having become dormant many weeks ago, but indoor plants struggle along from day to day trying to absorb any light rays that may strike their leaves during the brief period when the sun is up.

All plants are naturally solar powered, something we tend to forget as the houseplants that grew happily all summer long abruptly stop growing and flowering as the depths of winter approach. In the more southerly regions of Canada, the December sun is only about a fifth of what it was in the summer, while in the far north, the sun has been all but extinguished. With so little light, it's not surprising that most house and office plants are looking a lot like Charlie Brown's Christmas tree.

The gut reaction to sickly plants is to immediately begin administering a barrage of treatments ranging from fertilizer to sprays to soil drenches in a misguided and futile attempt to reinvigorate what are simply sun-starved plants.

Plants that are hungry for light energy can only be satiated in a couple of ways. Either they can be provided with more sunlight, which can be achieved by moving them closer to a bright window, or grow lights can be installed to supplement the dwindling sunlight and return the plants to their former grandeur. Installing grow lights would seem to be a simple and straight-forward solution, but the problem is a bit trickier to solve than it first appears.

Plants will use pretty much the entire rainbow of visible light for growth, but they do have a preference for blue and red light. Green light is not used to the same degree as red and blue, and most of it is reflected, which is why leaves appear green to our eyes. Grow-light manufacturers produce bulbs with a higher proportion of red and blue light to suit plants' needs. So, the solution to the light problem in the home appears rather simple: unscrew the existing bulbs and replace them with grow lights.

But the problem with grow lights lies not in the spectrum of light they emit but rather in the total amount of usable light they are capable of producing. All of the correct colours are present, but there's just too small a quantity of each colour of light to have a substantial impact on plant growth! It's comparable to painting an enormous rainbow on a wall but having only a thimble full of each colour of paint.

Yet there are highly specialized grow lights available that are not only capable of emitting the best spectrum of colours for plant growth but also pack a powerful punch of light. They are called high-intensity discharge lights, or HID lights for short. HID lights are designed to convert as much of the electrical energy that goes into the lamp into light that can be utilized by plants. Inefficient lights, like incandescents and even some poor-quality grow lights, convert the lion's share of electrical energy into heat rather than light. Heat without light causes plants to become soft and weak.

So why not simply replace incandescent bulbs with HID lights and have a domestic tropical jungle year-round?

Well, the overwhelming problem with HIDs is cost: both the purchase price and the electrical bill can be rather prohibitive. HID lights can run several hundred dollars for the combination of the bulb and the specialized fixture that must be used to house it. And although HID lights are very efficient at converting electrical energy to light energy, they still require a fair bit of current to do their job properly. Besides, the light is so intense that anyone sitting near an HID bulb would either be constantly squinting or relegated to wearing sunglasses, and the bulb's glow is often an eerie orange-yellow that renders any vibrantly coloured objects dull and flat.

Other than sunlight, nothing matches HID lights for stimulating plant growth, but because of their cost and intensity, they are really only suitable for solariums that need supplemental light or for growing particularly high-value plants—hopefully *legal* high-value plants!—in rooms devoid of sunlight.

We use HID lights in the greenhouse to encourage the growth of several tropical or semi-tropical plants like mandevilla that would otherwise languish during our short December days. Rose growers typically use HIDs to boost cut-flower production. Plants are often incapable of flowering during the winter simply because flowers are voracious consumers of plant energy, and the leaves are unable to match the demand. Under low light, plants will abruptly drop flowers to reduce the drain on their valuable energy resources. HID lights rather effectively reverse this tendency.

Supplementary lights aren't essential for the winter survival of houseplants, but every extra bit helps. But don't forget to use sunlight to the fullest. It's free and readily accessible, so it's better to relocate the windowsill figurines for a couple of months and give the plants their day in the sun. Clean your windows thoroughly—even relatively clean windows will still reflect up to 10% of the incoming sunlight. And don't worry about the new generation of windows that reflect ultraviolet light. UV light has very little effect on plant growth.

Christmas is a time when many people seek spiritual enlightenment. For plants, the need for enlightenment is much more basic.

on advances in geranium breeding...

Non-shattering flowers • Wide range of colours • Superb weather tolerance

GERANIUMS ARE SO POPULAR THAT I COULDN'T GO WITHOUT WRITING
AT LEAST ONE ARTICLE THAT EXAMINED THEIR HISTORY. I STILL GROW BOTH
SEED AND VEGETATIVE GERANIUMS, AND I LOVE THEM BOTH. I HOPE THIS STORY
WILL INDUCE AFICIONADOS OF ONE FORM OR THE OTHER TO TRY THEIR
OPPOSITE NUMBER; BOTH TYPES HAVE MUCH TO OFFER.

The Secret Lives of Geraniums

✻ ORIGINALLY PUBLISHED MARCH 13, 1999 ✻

Geraniums have long been one of my most beloved flowers. Their vibrant blooms and large round heads are seductive to many. In fact, I've often been cornered by panicky geranium lovers, seeking the seed of the big, lush specimen they spotted in their neighbour's garden. Unfortunately, all too frequently I'm forced to serve as the bearer of bad tidings, because many geranium varieties can't be grown from seed. A great deal of the geraniums we enjoy today are very specialized plants that have a hard time reproducing without the human touch.

Geranium aficionados know that there are two main types: seed geraniums and vegetative geraniums. It's easy to spot the differences between the two. Seed geraniums are usually smaller and less vigorous, and are sold in packs. My friend Jean Irwin swears by seed geraniums, often buying one hundred at a time for mass plantings.

They're pretty but inexpensive. Vegetative geraniums, on the other hand, are bigger, bushier plants, with more striking blooms. Another friend, Ellen Manson, buys nothing but vegetative geraniums, calling seed varieties "unspectacular." She wants the bigger blooms and bushier foliage, not caring about the higher cost. As it turns out, the origins of these plants are as strikingly different as people's reasons for loving them.

In 1632, the first geranium relative was shipped from South Africa to England. Over the next few years, dozens of *Pelargonium* species were taken from their South African homes to greenhouses and conservatories all over Europe. Today's zonal geraniums, *Pelargonium xhortum*, have a common source: they are the result of hybridization of *P. inquinans* and *P. zonale*, two of the South African immigrants. Until 1880, all zonal geraniums were diploids, meaning that they had eighteen chromosomes. During that year, a spontaneous mutation occurred in one plant, that doubled the number of chromosomes to 36, yielding a geranium called a tetraploid. The new arrival had stems and flowers that were considerably larger and more robust than its predecessors. However, tetraploids are much less fertile than diploids, and when they do manage to reproduce, the offspring are rarely true to type. Thus, the new tetraploids could only be reproduced by taking cuttings from the mutant and then taking still more cuttings after the first cuttings matured.

We continue to provide that help today. In greenhouses and gardens all over the world, a healthy part of a mother plant is snipped off and replanted, creating a perfect genetic duplicate of the original—a clone. Although long the stuff of science fiction and only recently popularized by Dolly the sheep, cloning has been a part of gardening since the first time some clever person pulled a shoot from a favourite plant and gave it to a friend to grow somewhere else.

These days, of course, our methods are a little more sophisticated. You can take a cutting from any geranium to produce a clone. However, the one in your backyard probably isn't the best candidate for a quality cutting, mainly because in the garden environment, disease and viruses can infect the mother plant. Such infections are often passed on to the clone. More rarely, viruses can trigger a mutation, changing the mother plant's DNA—which is also passed on to any cuttings. Gardeners are often disappointed when their cuttings turn out to be pale shadows of the original plant. Like bad photocopies, they don't recapture the glory of the original.

To avoid this problem, plant breeders use a method called mass clonal systems. The four-stage process involves subjecting a group of source plants to a series of inspections and disease treatments. The method insures that the stock plants that emerge from the system are all vigorous, disease-free, true-to-type specimens. These stock plants supply the cuttings that retail greenhouses use to grow the geraniums you buy in the store. To date, hundreds of tetraploids have been cultivated, including popular favourites like the 'Designer' geranium series.

Seed geraniums are propagated very differently. In the 1960s, Penn State University introduced the first commercial seed-propagated zonal geranium, a variety called 'Nittany Lion.' Varieties like the Nittany Lion or today's 'Pinto' series are the hybrid offspring of two distinct diploid parents—let's call them A and B. A was inbred for several generations to produce a very uniform parent. The same was done for B. Establishing parent blocks made it possible to breed offspring with the best traits of the parents. A, for example, might have big, beautiful blooms but dull colour. Parent B, on the other hand, might have smaller blooms but an intense, vibrant colour. A and B are then crossed to produce seed for an F1 hybrid—an offspring that combines the big flowers of parent A with the brilliant colour of parent B. The F1 hybrid will produce seed, but because it's a hybrid, if its seed is collected and grown the following spring, the resulting plants will look like parents (or grandparents) A and B, and not like the F1 parent. Since hybrid geraniums are so poor at reproducing themselves, Parent A and Parent B can rest assured that they have permanent jobs as pampered breeding stock. ("Nice work if you can get it," some might say.)

With all the fuss over cloning and genetic engineering these days, I think it's important to step back and get a little perspective. The practice of grafting trees to different rootstock was once punishable as an offence against God, but no one thinks anything of it today. Like it or not, humans are part of the ecosystem, and our "interference," it could be argued, is perfectly natural. Of course, we must use our capabilities responsibly—humans have been responsible for a great number of ecological disasters. But if human efforts can create something as beautiful as a Designer geranium—well, we can't be all that bad.

THIS ARTICLE WAS A REAL JOY TO WRITE. IT WAS COMPLETED IN DIRECT
RESPONSE TO A LETTER I RECEIVED FROM A HUSBAND AND WIFE WHO WERE
HAVING TROUBLE WITH ONE OF THOSE "TOMATO TREES" YOU OFTEN SEE IN
ADS. AND NOW I'M GETTING QUESTIONS ABOUT AN INDOOR BANANA TREE
THAT, LIKE THE TOMATO TREE, SOUNDS JUST A LITTLE TOO GOOD TO BE TRUE.
SOUNDS LIKE A LITTLE MORE SCIENTIFIC INVESTIGATION IS CALLED FOR...

You Say Tomato...But Is It?

⚜ ORIGINALLY PUBLISHED JANUARY 9, 1999 ⚜

It's not unusual for me to receive letters from gardeners who
have been experiencing difficulties. Most of the problems are routine. But last month I received a letter that reminded me how some
background in the science behind plants can really come in
handy—and how important it is to examine your philosophy
towards gardening.

You've probably seen television and print ads for a "miracle
plant" called a tomato tree. The ads show a smiling farmer holding
up a basket overflowing with enormous beefsteak tomatoes, while
a nearby drawing of the tomato tree implies that it was the source
of this bountiful harvest. The ad claims that the tree will produce

60 pounds of fruit each year, promising "bushel after bushel of mouth watering flavor—up to 7 months outdoors and all year round indoors." Well, who could resist such an appealing plant? The folks who wrote to me certainly couldn't.

Unfortunately, the tomato tree they received hasn't performed as advertised. The correspondents explained that they had grown their plant for 18 months, and while it evolved into a tall tree, it was very poor at branching out and the few blossoms that appeared quickly dropped off. From what I can tell from the information in the letter, these gardeners are doing everything correctly: they have the plant in the correct size of pot, and they're using the right fertilizer, pinching off the top growth to encourage branching out, and giving it plenty of water. Under these circumstances, one would think that the plant would produce fruit.

The key to the problem leapt out at me when I read one line: "We are told it is of the Solanum family–*Cyphomandra betacea*." Tomatoes are indeed of the Solanum family. So are potatoes, jimson weed, tobacco, and petunias. Botanical families are very large groupings of plants, most with an incredible number of diverse plant types within each one. To get a narrower grouping of more closely related plants, you need to look at the genus. The popular garden tomato belongs to genus *Lypersicon*–not *Cyphomandra*.

This simple revelation guarantees that the "tomato tree" will never produce garden-variety tomatoes. It may produce fruits that are similar...but they certainly won't be the beefsteaks pictured in the ad. According to our botanical encyclopedia, fruits from *Cyphomandra betacea* reach an average of only 5 cm in diameter— about the size of a typical cherry tomato. Not only that, these plants, like real tomatoes, are native to South America, so they share the same need for plenty of heat and sunshine. In most parts of Canada, that means three or four months of suitable weather at best, and the tree will struggle mightily to set fruit indoors, unless of course you have a greenhouse.

Even so, the tree stands a decent chance of producing fruit during the summer. In my reply, I told the frustrated gardeners to bathe their plant in sunlight. I suggested placing it against a south-facing wall and watering it every morning, with a pinch of 20-20-20 added to the watering can. I also noted that it's possible our northern climate has delayed fruit production. Some plants need a few years to set fruit for the first time, and the tomato tree may be having trouble adjusting to the cool Canadian summer nights. With any luck, their plant will eventually produce some fruit. I hope they write me back if they succeed, because I'd be interested in hearing how the fruits that appear compare to real tomatoes in taste and texture. Apparently, they are used for stewing in some regions of South America.

The problem of diminished expectations remains. To my mind, when you see an ad with a claim that seems too good to be true, you should ask yourself why the greenhouses in your area aren't growing and promoting the miracle plant in question. If the tomato tree performed as advertised, you can bet that I'd be pushing people to try it. (As it is, I'll stick to championing 'Tumbler' tomatoes.)

Even so, I encourage gardeners to be adventurous as long as their exuberance is tempered with just a dash of skepticism. You must be willing to take the good with the bad. Buying a plant from the wrong genus or species and not getting what you expect isn't the end of the world. Bruce Keith, an employee of mine, purchased a *Cyphomandra* a few years ago. He didn't get any fruit either, but he still feels that the tree was a worthwhile purchase. In Bruce's words, "I spent a couple of bucks and enjoyed a nice ornamental plant for a few months. It's like buying an orange tree up here. You don't buy it for the fruit, you buy it because it's pretty." I couldn't have said it better myself.

―――― BEST ADVICE ――――
on some of my priceless favourites...
The old bristlecone pine in St. Albert • The Ural peony by my house
• The huge elm at the end of my yard

WHEN BOB STADNYK, OUR PERENNIALS MANAGER, HEARD ABOUT A
UNIQUE $10,000 HOSTA, HE IMMEDIATELY ASKED BILL, "I'M SURE THE
ANSWER IS NO, BUT CAN I ORDER ONE OF THESE?" WELL, WE DIDN'T WIND
UP ORDERING THE HOSTA IN QUESTION, BUT I WAS INTRIGUED ENOUGH BY
BOB'S STORY TO SHARE IT WITH MY FELLOW GARDENERS.

The $10,000 Hosta

� ORIGINALLY PUBLISHED JANUARY 30, 1999 ✾

It's not unusual for collectors to pay thousands of dollars for an item
that they simply must have. A bottlecap from a 1920s Coke bottle, a rare
Koi fish, a Picasso original, old comic books, even a certain baseball hit
out of the St. Louis ballpark last year—to the right person, these items
take on a significance that transcends their "real" value.

Collectors also exist in the gardening world. It's not unusual for
enthusiasts to spend a hundred dollars or more for a single annual to
use as a focal point in the garden, for example. Or if they love roses,
they may be willing to spend double the regular price—perhaps
$40 instead of $20—for a particularly striking or unusual variety.

Even the most avid plant collector might be given pause, however, by a $10,000 price tag. What kind of plant could be worth that
much? A very special hosta, one our perennials manager Bob
Stadnyk heard about not too long ago.

The hosta in question was a hybrid plant. Hybrids have been engineered by humans to possess the positive characteristics of two or more parent plants. (Of course, hybrids occur in nature, too, as part of the natural process of evolution.) Every year, thousands of scientists cross millions of plants, aiming to create the ultimate rose or tulip or any other plant you can name. Breeders are looking for specific traits: better disease and pest resistance, bigger leaf and flower size, different maturity time, increased flower quantity, weather resistance, specific colours, different growth habit, ease of culture, and other, more esoteric qualities. Edible hybrid crops often possess superior flavour and storage characteristics.

To bring plants with any of these desirable traits to market takes an enormous investment—and the more of the above traits a hybrid possesses, the more valuable the plant becomes. Breeders must grow thousands of crosses to ensure that even a few of the offspring plants do indeed develop the desirable trait or traits of the parents. Valuable greenhouse space is set aside, strict sanitation procedures are maintained, and thousands of hours of labour make each experiment a costly prospect. Many years can be spent simply waiting for a plant to grow to maturity. Naturally, this means that the plant must be maintained over that period of time.

When a hybrid is deemed suitable for the market, breeders start propagating the plant. During the early stages of a hybrid's introduction, there may only be a limited number of plants available—and supply and demand dictates that scarce, desirable plants are more expensive than more commonly available varieties. If the plant is difficult to germinate or propagate, that drives the price even higher.

The $10,000 hosta possessed many of the desirable hybrid traits. It was also very difficult to propagate: tissue culture wouldn't work, so the original hybrid turned out to be unique. With only one in existence, it's no wonder that its assessed value is so high. Unfortunately, this inability to create cheap copies of the plant means that despite its wonderful qualities, this hosta is pretty much a dead end as far as commercial production goes. Bob jokes that the original plant is probably sitting in the garden of the CEO of the breeding company. Another employee of mine, Jan Goodall, speculates that the breeder chose not to propagate the hosta so that its value would remain high. The prestige of owning a very rare item may sometimes be enough to dissuade breeders from propagating plants.

The prestige factor is definitely at work in the case of Japanese double hepaticas. The Japanese love these plants! They have plenty of fully double, pom-pom-like flowers, and they are very lush and full; they are also quite hardy. These traits make the new hepaticas very desirable, and that desirability has pushed the price up to 4,000 to 6,000 yen per plant—or about 500 Canadian dollars! Canadian retailers are having a hard time importing Japanese double hepaticas right now; the few Japanese suppliers don't give up these rare beauties easily. Sometimes a trade will work better than cash: rare North American plants are occasionally exchanged for the hepaticas. The barter system is alive and well, at least when it comes to getting a hold of exotic flora.

Most peonies cost about $18. There is a new hybrid peony, however, that costs about $90. It's the first cross between a tree peony and a herbaceous peony, and it's just gorgeous. It looks like a regular peony except for the flower colour: these peonies are yellow with red centres. Like the hosta and the double hepatica, this peony is the result of thousands of hours of work. It's not quite as expensive partly because it's been somewhat more successful; it's been bred in large quantities and it's not terribly difficult to propagate. It's still more expensive than most plants, however, and that's because of everyday costs that retailers incur during the course of obtaining the plants. These costs include shipping, customs fees, agricultural fees (inspections, etc.), export permits, phytosanitary permits, and exchange rates.

In light of the intensive labour involved in creating these spectacular hybrid varieties, it has to be said that the finished plants are works of art as wonderful as any symphony. The inspiration and delight they provide really is priceless.

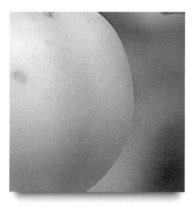

THIS IS ONE OF MY FAVOURITE ARTICLES BECAUSE I JUST MAY HAVE
HELPED TO SAVE A SPECIES THAT COULD HAVE BECOME EXTINCT. MANY
OBSCURE VARIETIES OF PLANTS FACE EXTINCTION EVERY YEAR, BUT THANKS
TO JIM, GENEVIEVE STOKOWSKI, AND DR. IEUAN EVANS, A VALUABLE PEAR
MAY SOON BE A LITTLE MORE COMMONPLACE IN ALBERTA YARDS.

A Pear of Great Price

⸎ ORIGINALLY PUBLISHED AUGUST 28, 1999 ⸎

Last month, I received a desperate phone call from Genevieve
Stokowski, an Edmonton gardener. "Lois, I have a pear tree in my
back yard that produces exquisite fruit. My father planted it years
ago, and it's not a variety that you can buy at any of the nurseries.
I'm afraid that when it dies, we'll have lost a wonderful pear forever." Genevieve wasn't concerned about saving the tree for herself–
rather, she wanted to ensure that the tree's remarkable characteristics could be shared with future generations.

She explained that her father had given the tree its start back
in the 1940s, grafting a pear branch onto the trunk of an apple tree
in the back yard. Genevieve recalls how skeptical her brother was
when the spindly branch was bound to the narrow trunk. "Never
you mind," her father said, confident that the graft would take–and

it did. For years now, the tree has been producing heavy yields of exceptionally sweet and juicy fruit. My son Jim visited Genevieve to look at the tree in May, and he commented on its remarkable size and vigour. He described a huge, vibrant specimen, covered with blossoms.

However, every tree must die eventually. While Genevieve's pear is still in excellent health, it can't last forever. Something needed to be done to preserve the tree's unique traits. We decided to contact Ieuan Evans, a great gardener and friend who serves as a plant pathologist for Alberta Agriculture. Ieuan has a passion for fruit trees: he discovered and propagated a popular, prolific cherry tree that bears his namesake today, the Evans cherry. His interest fired, Ieuan and a colleague promptly headed out to Genevieve's house in east Edmonton and took a few branches (or scions, as they are referred to by horticulturists). They then grafted those scions to some sturdy rootstock. To give the pear the best chance of long-term survival, Ieuan also distributed a few scions to a number of fruit growers and home gardeners. With any luck, this excellent pear will thrive in Alberta orchards and yards for many, many years to come.

Genevieve's tree is probably an heirloom variety–a pristine, natural source of valuable genetic material. Genevieve's father grew up in Poland, and though she couldn't confirm whether his pear came from Poland, too, it's highly likely that it did. Sharing plants and branches was common in the Polish community, and the pear in question was probably brought to Canada by one of Mr. Stokowski's friends—making it rare indeed in this country. This rarity, combined with its delicious fruit and heavy yields, made the tree an obvious candidate for preservation. However, many varieties with less apparent qualities deserve to be saved, too.

Take, for example, an old pear tree that produces poor fruit, but never dies back, no matter how severe the winter. The tree is still a valuable genetic resource—its hardiness traits can be selected and interbred with, say, a tender tree with excellent fruit. Ideally, a hardy tree with delicious fruit will be the end result—a result that would not have been possible had the "inferior" heirloom been allowed to die out.

There's a story about corn that illustrates perfectly the importance of preserving as many wild or heirloom plants as possible. Corn is descended from a wild Mexican grass called *teosinte*. Thousands of years of crossbreeding by farmers ancient and modern produced the plants we grow and love today. (Indeed, modern corn cannot grow without human intervention.) In 1977, an undergraduate student from the University of Guadalajara discovered a new species of *teosinte*. He stumbled across the find in the cloud forests of the Sierra de Manantlan near Guadalajara and Puerto Vallarta. While the *teosinte* was unremarkable at first glance, studies revealed that the newly discovered species possessed genes resistant to seven of the nine major corn diseases. More importantly, for five of the seven, no other sources for resistant genes are known. The *teosinte* in question grows only in three small areas of Mexico, totalling less than two hundred hectares of space. Had the student not made the discovery, it is all too likely that spreading developments like farms and ranches would have overrun the fields. Thankfully, the University of Guadalajara created a nature reserve to save this rare, valuable species.

Saving heirloom plants has another, less obvious benefit. As agricultural corporations get larger and larger, control over the best plant varieties becomes concentrated in the hands of fewer and fewer people. While I agree that corporations do valuable breeding work and should receive financial compensation for their research, there's something troubling about the idea that one day one or two companies might "own" most of the best varieties.

But plants found in the wild cannot be patented and sold as developed varieties can—at least, not without considerable legal wrangling. Genevieve's pear tree will now become part of the public domain. It can be grown strictly for its superior characteristics or used as breeding stock for the development of new pear varieties. The important point is that its gene pool will live on—hopefully forever.

Old heirloom varieties have become more, not less, important as our science advances. That old tree in your backyard may be more than an ugly, ragged eyesore: it may contain genes as old as the hills that possess characteristics of worth beyond measure.

I'm excited about the future of gardening, but it doesn't hurt to hang onto a little slice of the past. Indeed, Genevieve's next door neighbour just called to tell me about her unique, amazing cherry tree...

——— BEST ADVICE———
on great Canadian plants...
Saskatoons • Explorer roses • Evans cherry

WHEN I CAUGHT THE SCENT OF THE CINNAMITE AD
MENTIONED IN THIS ARTICLE, I SMELLED A STORY—IF YOU'LL
PARDON THE PUN. NOT ONLY DID IT GIVE ME THE CHANCE TO
COMMENT ON A POTENTIALLY USEFUL NEW PRODUCT, BUT I WAS ALSO
ABLE TO EXPLAIN THE COMPLEX BUT NECESSARY PROCEDURES THAT
FOREIGN PESTICIDES GO THROUGH TO GAIN ACCESS TO CANADIAN MARKETS.

Cautious Canadians

⚜ ORIGINALLY PUBLISHED JUNE 5, 1999 ⚜

Picture if you will a sweat-stained farmer in his field, his trousers stained with spilled chemicals. He wipes his grubby hands on his pants...and his trousers suddenly burst into flame. He frantically beats out the fire, quickly enough so that the only casualties are his scorched jeans and his equally singed dignity. Spontaneous combustion? No, it's not an episode of the *X-Files*; it's something that happened all too frequently back in the 1950s. Some farmers were a little sloppy with a herbicide called sodium chlorate, spilling it on their clothing. The chemical in question is very flammable when dry, and the friction generated by rubbing hands against chemical-soaked pants was explosive.

Sodium chlorates are rarely used today; newer, safer products have replaced them. In fact, Canadian authorities would probably not register products like sodium chlorate these days: regulations are much more stringent. But while modern regulations save us from unfortunate incidents like the one described above, they may also be keeping some worthwhile pest-control products out of our backyards.

For example: a few weeks ago I came across an intriguing ad for a product called Cinnamite. The ad included a "scratch 'n' sniff" sticker, which I dutifully scratched. The smell was extremely pleasant—a strong cinnamon odour. It turns out that this smell that so delighted my senses is purportedly capable of wiping out mites within minutes. Most interestingly, though, Cinnamite smells like cinnamon because it *is* cinnamon—it's a natural product, the same stuff that's used to flavour doughnuts and pastries. I called up the company that makes Cinnamite, a firm in Butte, Montana called Mycotech. A technical advisor explained to me that the Cinnamite is merely an extract of cinnamon oil and that certain chemicals in the extract, called flavonoids, have insecticidal properties. (The common organic insecticide known as Rotenone is related to the flavonoids.) The product has already become popular in its country of origin, the United States. Growers there enjoy its zero-day preharvest interval (that is, the property that makes it safe to consume shortly after spraying).

So when can we expect this safe, effective, natural product to be available in Canada? It could be a while. Apparently, registering agricultural products in Canada is more trouble than it's worth for some companies. The Mycotech official explained that the potential market for Cinnamite in Central America, for example, is probably four times that in Canada, and their registration process takes only months. It takes years to register new pesticides here— even pesticides made from natural products, like Cinnamite.

In the United States, all pesticides are rigorously investigated for harmful side effects on "non-target" animals like ducks, pigs, fish, and so on. However, there isn't an official US government stamp of approval for efficacy. As long as a pesticide can be shown to fit within the parameters of environmental and human health, it can be legally sold. However, there's no guarantee that it will work. The attitude below the 49th Parallel is that if the product doesn't meet the expectation of the consumer, the marketplace will determine whether the product survives.

In Canada, pesticide tests parallel those in the US. Here, however, the list of non-target organisms tested is a little broader, and tested pesticides also face one additional hurdle: they have to prove their effectiveness before they are approved for sale here. Consequently, it takes longer to register a product in Canada than it does in many other countries, and as a result it is also more costly for the company applying for registration.

Companies weigh the time and cost to register their products in Canada against the potential market (rather small here) and often decide not to pursue Canadian registration. If truth be known, I like our cautious, typically Canadian approach to pesticides—checking and rechecking to be relatively certain that the product is safe. However, I do worry that some very safe products might never see the light of day in Canada simply because there's little profit in getting them registered here. There are indications, though, that certain environmentally friendly products, like Cinnamite, are likely to receive somewhat streamlined treatment by Canadian officials in the near future.

I think our flaming farmer would be content with the present situation. It may take a little longer for certain products to get into gardeners' hands these days, but the added safety factor makes them worth the wait. And at least you won't ignite when using Cinnamite.

—— BEST ADVICE ——
on plants I'm waiting to see...
True yellow impatiens • Black tulip • Blue rose

HAVE YOU EVER WONDERED ABOUT THE BRILLIANT FOLKS
WHO DEDICATE THEIR LIVES TO BREEDING NEW PLANT VARIETIES?
OR BETTER STILL, HAVE YOU EVER WANTED TO BE AMONG THEIR NUMBER?
THE STORIES BEHIND THE AMAZING PLANTS WE ENJOY IN TODAY'S
GARDENS ARE OFTEN JUST AS CAPTIVATING AS THE PLANTS THEMSELVES.
IT WAS MY PRIVILEGE TO KNOW ROBERT SIMONET, AND I WAS HAPPY
TO PAY TRIBUTE TO HIS PIONEERING GENIUS IN THIS ARTICLE.

The Gardeners
of the Golden Age

✢ ORIGINALLY PUBLISHED JUNE 13, 1998 ✢

Every time I walk into my garden, I am confronted by plants that
I could never have imagined ten or twenty years ago. Cool Breeze
cucumbers, Explorer roses...new varieties are popping up all the
time. As far as I'm concerned, this is the Golden Age of gardening.
But all of this splendour didn't spring up on its own; hard-working
men and women spent years creating these spectacular plants.
Whenever I have a chance to reflect on the work of these pioneers,
I think about Robert Simonet.

Robert Simonet was probably one of the nicest people I've ever met. Ted and I first encountered him in the 1960s, back during the early days of our gardening business. We bought our strawberry and petunia seeds from Bob, and driving out to his Sherwood Park home just east of Edmonton was always a pleasure. We'd sit down at the kitchen table and he'd bring out coffee cans full of seeds. Bob didn't use scales or any other fancy equipment; he'd just use a measuring spoon to scoop up the seed, shake the scoop to level off the mound, and finally dump what was left into a brown paper bag. Somehow, that always turned out to be the right amount. After this ritual was complete, we would all sit down for coffee and conversation—but my favourite part of the visit was when he would take us out to his greenhouse to show off the gorgeous varieties of rutabaga and everbearing strawberries that he had created. Bob was a first-rate plant breeder. I was even more impressed with his talent when I discovered that he was self-taught. He never did attend university formally; instead, he used the university library to learn about botany and plant breeding.

Bob's most famous discovery came during the dark years of World War Two. When you think about this terrible time, gardening isn't usually the first thing that springs to mind, but war has many ways of stealing beauty from the world. Before the war, only the expert botanists of the Empire of Japan held the secret of producing double-flowering petunias. It was a secret they guarded jealously; no one outside Japan had any idea how they did it. Anyone who wanted to grow double petunias had to buy the seed from them. After the outbreak of hostilities, of course, all trade with Japan was cut off—meaning that double petunia seed was completely unavailable to the rest of the world. These beautiful flowers seemed lost forever.

But Bob couldn't let that happen. Using all of the knowledge and skill at his command, he cracked the mystery and discovered how to grow double petunias from seed before the end of the war, to the surprise and delight of Allied gardeners everywhere—and to the shock and dismay of Imperial Japan. Incredible! It may seem like a small thing, compared to the more famous earth-shaking events of that time, but to my mind Robert Simonet made a very important contribution to the war effort. Indeed, many of the gorgeous double-flowering petunias available today were created by Bob.

Unfortunately, Bob received very little financial compensation for the years of heroic effort he put into creating these new varieties. While I'm sure that wasn't foremost in his mind when he rediscovered the double petunia, I think it's important for these innovative creators to be rewarded for their work. At the very least, they should have an opportunity to recover their costs. These days, more breeders are becoming aware of a relatively new way to recoup the costs of research and development: patent protection.

In Canada, new cultivars can be registered with the Plant Breeders' Rights Office of the Canadian Food Inspection Agency. But not just any new variety will be granted copyright protection. To satisfy the PBRO requirements, new plant varieties must have four characteristics:

1. they must be new;
2. they must be distinct;
3. they must be uniform; and,
4. they must be stable.

In brief, "new" means that the plant must not have been made available for sale prior to the application for PBRO protection. "Distinct" means that the plant must be measurably different than previous varieties in at least one way, such as colour, growth habit, disease resistance, and so on. "Uniform" means that any variations in the plant's characteristics must be predictable to the extent that they can be described by a breeder, or they must fall within a commercially acceptable range. Finally, "stable" means that the variety must remain true to its description over successive generations. The 'Designer' geranium is a good example of a new plant that's met all of these criteria–the chief distinction being that this series of geraniums sports new colour patterns that have never been seen before. The 'White Fire' geranium is perhaps the most stunning of these, with white flowers complemented by hot-pink eyes. It is, of course, stable, uniform, and new, as well.

After the applicant's plant has been thoroughly tested to see whether it meets these requirements, patent protection may be granted. If the application is successful, the breeder is granted certain rights, including:

1. the right to produce and sell the propagating material of the protected variety;
2. the right to make repeated use of the protected plant as a step to producing another variety commercially;
3. the right to make repeated use of the protected variety for production of ornamental plants or cut-flowers; and,
4. the right to license a third party (such as a greenhouse) to any of the above acts, with or without conditions.

There are restrictions to the patent holder's rights, as well. For example, anyone may use a protected variety to breed and develop new plant varieties.

All kinds of breeders have been granted patent protection for their creations, from large industrial concerns to observant backyard horticulturists who have managed to create new varieties almost by accident. The beautiful thing about patent protection is that it protects the little guy as much as it does the big corporations.

(By the way, plants found growing in the wild are not eligible for patent protection: they belong to all of us. You can't patent that oak tree out on your granddad's farm, for example, or Alberta's wild rose.)

Once a breeder has secured a patent, he can collect royalties for each propagation of that plant. At our greenhouse, for example, we sell the gorgeous new 'Forest Flame' nasturtiums. For each reproduction we make of the plant, we must pay a royalty to the company that created this variety. These payments help offset the expense of producing these beautiful plants, and they also fund further research into producing more new varieties.

While I'm sure that the vast majority of growers dutifully pay their royalties, the temptation to make illegal copies of plants is so great that there must be hundreds of thousands of "pirated plants" being sold to unwary consumers every year. When this happens, there is less incentive for breeders to create new varieties, and those that they do produce will have to be more expensive to offset the costs of piracy. Imagine not being able to enjoy the abundant and delicious Tumbler tomato...or the convenience and versatility of dwarf apple trees.

If we want to keep enjoying the fruits of progress from plant breeding, we should do all we can to support the efforts of these gardening pioneers, especially the independent breeders. Often it is the success of the independents that spurs the larger companies on to experiment. In the future, we may see wonders like blue roses or peaches that will grow in Whitehorse—but only if we show that we are willing to recognize and compensate our researchers. So the next time you're watering that lush purple carpet of Wave petunias, stop and think for a moment about Robert Simonet and all of the other breeders like him. Who knows? Perhaps one day you'll join their ranks.

———Best Advice———
on great tree care ideas...
Pole pruner • Recycled rubber rings for tree bases • Once-a-year fertilizer spikes

Boulevard of Dreams

꙲ ORIGINALLY PUBLISHED SEPTEMBER 18, 1999 ꙲

THE IMPETUS FOR THIS ARTICLE CAME WHEN A PERSON BROUGHT IN A
BOULEVARD TREE WITH A ROOT BALL GIRDLED BY A NYLON CORD. THE CORD
COULD ONLY HAVE BEEN LEFT THERE AS THE RESULT OF CARELESSNESS, AND
THE INDIGNATION I FELT FORCED ME TO EXAMINE WHAT COULD BE DONE TO
IMPROVE THE HEALTH OF CITY-MAINTAINED TREES.

A city that has boulevards lined with vigorous, healthy trees tells
me something about that place: it tells me that its citizens care about
beauty and the environment. A stately procession of big, beautiful
elms or maples lining the streets takes my breath away. But I've
come to realize that these trees are not just the city's responsibility.

Back in August, our son Bill saw that some well-established
boulevard trees up the road still had braces on them—long after the
trees could stand on their own. Fortunately, Bill noticed the braces
just as they were beginning to cut into the bark. A quick phone call
to inform the city's parks department solved the problem. The end-
less profusion of cords and straps wrapped around the trunks and
branches of young boulevard trees is a definite problem. These
devices look harmless, but they're killers. Christmas lights are lovely
on outdoor trees, but the straps that hold the strings of lights in
place must be removed each year. Leaving these straps on the trees

makes it easier to hang the lights every year, but as the tree grows, the straps inevitably cut the circulation to the branches, ensuring premature death.

We must realize that planting trees is just the first step. Diligent maintenance is just as important as proper planting. While limited city budgets and honest misconceptions can make it difficult to provide long-term care to boulevard trees, regular upkeep and a little common sense can preserve a community's investment. Several practices contribute to the downfall of boulevard trees, but a little care and planning on our part can ensure that they have a long and healthy life.

One practice that countless boulevard trees are subjected to is the relentless torture by weedeaters. Trees appear so tough and sturdy that many people don't realize the extent to which these buzzing devils can damage trees. Young trees are particularly vulnerable: the snapping cord of the weedeater slashes through and injures the thin cambium (the layer of bark responsible for growth) very easily. The damage is easy to spot: it manifests as a raised circle that girdles the trunk. Weedeater wounds can stunt growth, make trees more vulnerable to insects and disease, or kill them outright. It is simple to prevent such wounds. Just allowing the grass to grow a little taller around your boulevard trees can eliminate the problem, although many people think this looks unkempt. A plastic collar or a circular bed of annuals around the trunk can solve the problem, too. In the short term, it's an expensive solution, but far less expensive than replacing the tree.

Like any trees, boulevard trees need regular pruning. If left to their own devices, many trees develop weak branches attached to the main body of the tree at dangerously narrow angles. Unless they are pruned at the appropriate time, these branches may snap off during a strong wind and expose the trunks to insect and disease pests. Most cities have excellent pruning programs, but occasionally a tree or two gets missed. If a tree look particularly neglected it might be worthwhile calling the city's parks department.

Construction is a necessary evil in cities but can cause severe damage to nearby trees. A magnificent 80-year-old silver maple that I drive past regularly is surely doomed: a couple of years ago I watched, horrified, as construction crews tore up the earth around it to put in parking spots. The idea was to create a few lovely shaded spots under the tree, but at least one of the tree's largest roots was severed during construction. Ironically, the soil preparation for that pristine circle of asphalt will likely cause the tree to crash on top of the cars parked beneath its huge canopy.

Most Canadian cities are forced to use salt on the roads to increase traction in the winter. Unfortunately, salt usage has a number of disadvantages, including tree damage. Whenever a snowplow dumps a load of brown mush onto the boulevard, the ground beneath absorbs the salts, cutting off root absorption of water—while larger trees have a sufficiently extensive root system to evade salts, young trees don't. In our area, a related problem is the all-too-common practice of homeowners dumping sump pump water—high in sodium salts onto the soil around boulevard trees. Saline sump water should never be dumped around the base of trees.

Sometimes, a tree's poor health can be traced back to the day it was planted. On one street close to home, there's a long line of superb lindens—but every August, their leaves turn an ugly brown. Since this occurs during hot weather, there's a tendency to blame the change on high temperatures. However, closer inspection reveals that the trees were planted in small holes cut into the sidewalk. Removing a chunk of concrete and planting into a little hole with compacted clay leaves little room for roots to expand and absorb water. The loss of moisture through the leaves far outstrips the capacity of the confined roots to draw in water. During periods of drought, the leaves invariably turn brown, severely weakening the tree.

Fortunately, awareness of the importance of maintaining city trees is growing. Just a few months ago, a venerable and rare horse chestnut smack in the middle of downtown Edmonton made the news when a concerned horticulturist noted that the paving recently installed around the stately old tree would surely kill it. A group of concerned citizens raised enough cash to remove the pavement and re-landscape, saving the chestnut and beautifying the whole area. Many citizens contributed time and money to the project; my family donated lilies. I hope this story reflects a growing concern about the plants that are so very important to a city's image. It's everyone's job to look out for their health.

─── BEST ADVICE ───
on fantastic Japanese imports...
Profusion zinnias • Crystal Bowl Supreme pansies • Fantasy linaria

FROM 1998 TO 2000, I SERVED AS THE UNIVERSITY OF ALBERTA'S
CHANCELLOR, AND IT WAS ONE OF THE HIGHLIGHTS OF MY LIFE. WHILE
VISITING JAPAN ON U OF A BUSINESS, I HAD THE OPPORTUNITY TO TAKE A
CLOSE LOOK AT HOW THE JAPANESE APPROACH GARDENING. THE TRIP WAS FULL
OF DELIGHTFUL SURPRISES—HOW COULD I NOT SHARE THOSE EXPERIENCES?

Another Approach

✣ ORIGINALLY PUBLISHED JUNE 26, 1999 ✣

As Chancellor of the University of Alberta, I'm often asked to
represent the University at special events. One of these was the
opening of the University's Sightlines art exhibit at Musashino Art
University in Tokyo. My original task was to introduce audiences in
Japan to this exhibition of new artwork by University of Alberta
students and staff, but when the organizers in Japan heard that I was
a gardener, they asked me to speak to a group of students at another
institution, Meiji University. Given how much Japanese culture has
influenced Canadian gardening, it was an opportunity I wasn't
about to turn down.

When I reached Japan, I couldn't help but notice the striking
difference in landscaping style. As we whizzed along the highway
from the airport to the hotel, I admired the long hedges of azaleas
that divided the north and southbound lanes. They were tall and

thick and absolutely immaculate, with gorgeous pink flowers in full bloom. I noted that interspersed with the azaleas were rows of orange marigolds, also in full bloom. To me, these seemed less formal than the azaleas–almost as if some daring soul had run across the highway and planted them to provide a little contrast to the imposing hedges. The narrow ditches along the road were left wild– another interesting contrast to the azaleas.

I also took note of the homes along the highway. The front-yard vegetable gardens were incredibly efficient: pole beans ran up fences and exterior walls, cole crops flourished where Canadians would put grass, and there were even potatoes, more densely planted than I've ever seen. These vegetable gardens were incredibly clean; not a single weed dared intrude upon these sacred spaces.

When I reached the hotel, I noticed wild grasses growing on the boulevard instead of a manicured lawn. The hotel garden was more in line with what I'd expected to see: rocks, Itoh peonies, lots of ponds and streams with fish darting to and fro, plenty of evergreens, and relatively few flowers. There were plenty of fresh flowers inside the hotel, though–massive bouquets with a diverse mix of flowers, not at all the stereotypical single flower in a petite vase we've been led by movies to expect on Japanese tables. (Using the washroom was interesting. The first time I went to wash my hands, I discovered that there were no towels of any kind to dry off with. My travelling companions explained that in Japan you carry along your own hand towel at all times.)

When my little entourage went out on a short tour, I came across some of the most beautiful orchids I've ever seen. They graced the tables of the many flower shops we visited in Tokyo–all of which, it seemed, taught flower arranging, as my interpreter pointed out. Manicured evergreens were abundant in the parks we passed, and street vendors selling bedding plants had clay pots over-flowing with petunias.

When the time came to address the students at Meiji, I told them that the most striking difference I'd noticed between the Canadian way of gardening and the Japanese approach to gardening is the use of space. In a typical Canadian garden, every patch of soil is filled up with plants. When I wander through a Japanese garden, I notice the open spaces, the mass plantings, the sand and rock. It's a more ho-listic and spiritual approach to gardening that evokes feelings of peace, serenity–and often wonder.

The way we prune, too, has changed thanks to the Japanese influence. As little as five years ago you would never have seen topiary outside of public botanical gardens. Today, Japanese-style topiaries are a much more common sight.

The plants we use are changing as well. Everyone in Canada loves flowers, but we're getting a little braver and bolder in the varieties of plants we're incorporating into our landscapes: ferns and grasses, foliage plants and cacti, and hardy alpines. Many Canadian gardens are adapting Japanese motifs into their garden by using Japanese-style stepping stones, statues, fountains, and lanterns.

The most striking reaction to my talk came when I showed the students a few slides, including one of a Tumbler tomato heavy with ripe red fruit. They all leaned forward in their seats when I told them about this amazing variety, which produces hundreds of juicy, delicious tomatoes on each plant. I wouldn't be surprised if pots full of Tumblers were already springing up on Japanese balconies. Given food prices in Japan, the Tumbler should be a big hit. After the talk, I spoke to several of the students individually, and nearly everyone had questions about container gardening, and the Tumbler in particular.

Just before I returned to Canada, I was interviewed by Japan's most influential women's magazine, *Mrs*. I was a little surprised that they wanted to talk to me, but apparently they were fascinated by the fact that a farm woman had been instituted as the titular head of a Canadian university. I was given the impression that such a thing would cause a sensation in Japan.

Back when we started our business, the number of Japanese plants we sold could be counted on the fingers of one hand. Today, there are hundreds of Japanese imports lining our shelves. Double hepaticas, jack-in-the-pulpits, ornamental ginger, peonies, woodland perennials, rhododendrons, hostas, evergreens, Floral Showers snapdragons, Pageant primulas, Big Smile sunflowers, Imperial pansies—those are just a few examples. Then there's the flowering kale and cabbage, and of course, bonsai—in fact, there's a lovely little bonsai growing just a few feet away from my desk!

This trip really reinforced my belief that cultural exchange is a powerful progressive force. Our countries would be much poorer without continuous exchange of ideas and values.

WHEN I WAS ACTIVELY INVOLVED IN RUNNING THE GREENHOUSE,
A BLIND COUPLE ASKED ME IF I WOULD MIND IF THEY TOUCHED THE PLANTS—
SINCE, ALONG WITH SCENT, THAT WAS HOW THEY COULD EXPERIENCE THEIR
BEAUTY. OF COURSE I DIDN'T MIND, SINCE I TOO LOVE
TO ENJOY ALL OF THE SENSORY DELIGHTS THE GARDEN HAS TO OFFER.

A Feast for the Senses

ᴥ ORIGINALLY PUBLISHED APRIL 24, 1999 ᴥ

My favourite gardens are those that provide a feast for the senses. The most magnificent gardens pay tribute to each and every one.

Sight is usually the sense first affected by the garden, and a spectacular array of flowers is guaranteed to please the eye. Three new introductions in the Celebration line of New Guinea impatiens dazzle vision with absolutely stunning colours: Electric Rose, Sangria, and Lavender Glow. These impatiens are among the most vibrant flowers I've ever seen and look spectacular in the garden, especially exploding from hanging baskets with their neon glow. If my sons are reading this, remember that Mother's Day is coming up, kids...

Fans of striped roses should take a look at George Burns, a lovely tender rose with striking red, pink, yellow, and cream-striped double blooms. Scentimental roses are double-bloomed and multicoloured, too: burgundy-red swirled with creamy white. Both roses provide lots of blooms with sharply delineated colours. My daughter-in-law is planting one of each in her garden this year.

We often smell a garden before we ever see it. Scent is purported to trigger memory more clearly and powerfully than any of the other senses. Certainly, nothing takes me back to my childhood faster than a whiff of rhubarb.

According to what I've heard from the sweet pea society in Britain, nothing can match the new Gwendoline sweet pea for fragrance. Gwendoline, winner of two awards at the UK's 1998 Royal Horticultural Trials, boasts gorgeous lilac-pink flowers and has been called the most strongly scented variety of the modern era. They're gorgeous, too: Gwendoline's pink blooms are very large and showy. This year I'm devoting an entire row to Gwendoline, rather than planting the usual mix of sweet peas.

Looking for fragrant perennials? I've always found pinks to be quite charming, and the new Raspberry Wine is no exception. The blue-tinted foliage and small raspberry-pink flowers are delightful, as is the spicy clove scent. Other new fragrant perennials include Mexican hyssop, with a refreshing mint aroma, and flowering oregano, an ornamental version of the popular culinary herb.

You might not expect to smell chocolate in the garden, but Chocolate Cosmos reproduces that unmistakable scent so accurately that it causes one's mouth to water. Coincidentally (but appropriately), the flowers are a rich chocolate-brown. I wouldn't suggest filling a bed with Chocolate Cosmos—the smell would probably be a little too reminiscent of a confectionery—but it makes a great novelty plant.

Vegetables remain my main gardening passion, chiefly because I love the taste of freshly harvested produce. I'm really looking forward to biting into the first Ball Beefsteak tomato of the fall. The huge 300–400-g fruit are exceptionally juicy and sweet for a beefsteak tomato; they're wonderful for sandwiches, pizzas, or even eating off the vine.

The sharp but sweet tang of a bell pepper is a special treat, and Early Sunsation Hybrid promises to excel in that regard. The big, blocky golden-yellow fruit are rumoured to be extra sweet. I look forward to giving Early Sunsation a taste test; our first harvest should occur in a few weeks. It will be interesting to see if Early Sensation displaces my current favourite, Spanish Spice, a thin-skinned, very sweet bell pepper that I've loved for years.

Fruit lovers should try the Honey Queen raspberry. This isn't your typical raspberry: the bush produces heavy yields of larger-than-average, golden-yellow, extremely juicy, mildly sweet berries. And they make terrific jam—my daughter-in-law conjures up a few jars every fall. (We have a deal: I wander through the twenty-five-foot row and pick, while she does the work in the kitchen.)

The sense of touch plays an especially important role in gardening. My hands are my most important gardening tools, and I love getting them dirty. There are plenty of plants that call out to be fondled and caressed. Lamb's ear is one of those plants that looks so soft and fuzzy that one can't resist touching it to see if it's as soft as its name suggests—and it is! Even more pleasant is mint. It feels exquisite and leaves the most wonderful scent on your hands. I love working with mint in the kitchen!

Of course, not all plants are eager to be touched. I've gotten more scratches than I can count from rosebushes and other thorny plants, but perhaps the most threatening plant I know of is the aptly named devil's walking stick. This intimidating shrub makes the perfect hedge if it's privacy you're looking for: the thorns are so numerous and razor-sharp that any would-be intruders will think twice before attempting entry. Devil's walking stick is great for fending off pests like deer, coyotes, cats, and even the occasional hooligan.

The sounds of the garden are subtle, but no less relaxing or revealing than its other characteristics. For me, the surest sign of a good, hot summer is when I hear the seedpods of caragana hedges snapping, going off like cooking popcorn, sending seeds flying. Perennial gas plants can be noisy, too. If you hold a match close to one on a still, muggy evening, the flammable oil emitted by the flowers will burst into flame with a soft pop. However, I think my favourite "loud" plant is the trembling aspen. Even the slightest breeze causes its leaves to shiver and tremble. I find the soft rustling extremely soothing.

After going to the extra effort of planting with all the senses in mind, here's what to do: wander through your garden at a leisurely pace. Smell it, taste it, touch it, watch it, listen to it. Feast on it. Enjoy it.

About the Author

Lois Hole and her family have been sharing their gardening knowledge through books, radio, television, and newspapers for over a decade. Lois' goal has always been to provide advice that goes beyond the superficial—practical tips with a solid foundation of science and hard-won experience. She is the author of eight bestselling books and the co-author, with her son Jim, of the first three volumes in the *Q&A* series.

Lois currently serves as Alberta's Lieutenant Governor and is therefore taking a less active role in the publishing business. However, she can still be found sharing advice and hugs with customers in the gardens and greenhouses operated by her husband Ted, sons Bill and Jim, and daughter-in-law Valerie.

HOLE'S

Publication Director ✻ Bruce Timothy Keith
Editor ✻ Leslie Vermeer
Book Design ✻ Gregory Brown
Additional Text ✻ Earl J. Woods
Cover Photograph ✻ Sima Khorrami